前　　言

总有一种感动无处不在……

总有一种情愫绕人心怀……

总有一种生活，在别处，闪烁着奇异的光芒……

这些触动人灵魂深处的感受在何处找寻？去仔细品味一篇好的散文吧。有人曾说："读一篇好的散文，如品香茗，留香唇齿，馨香绕怀……"

每当夜幕来临之时，沏上一杯香茶，挑选一本自己喜欢的散文，在柔和的灯光下静静品读。白日里所有的喧嚣、烦琐、不快皆抛于脑后，唯有文字的蛩音在耳畔轻响，于是便听见了一个个心灵的独语，或欢唱，或啜泣，或奔放，或黯然。有时如大海惊涛拍岸，有时如青山巍峨屹立，有时又如海风轻盈扶摇，有时却如溪流淙淙叮咚。春天里，能够听见窗外黑暗的夜色花开的声音；夏日里，能够听见墙角蟋蟀的吟唱；秋夜里，能够听见郊外瓜果坠地的欢歌；充满诗意的冬日里，能够听见雪花落在窗台上忧郁的叹息……

那一刻，读书让我们在知性中享受更多的生活乐趣……

让我们邂逅那种从未见过却早就印在我们心底的生活方式……

让我们感受"看庭前花开花落，望天上云卷云舒"恬淡如菊的心境……

本书精选的50篇哲理散文，融语言美、意境美于一体。它们有的语言凝练，言简意赅，有的叙述详尽，丝丝入扣，其内容涉及生活的方方面面。本书里的故事会使您爱得博大深沉，活得充满激情；会使您满怀信心地去追求梦想与憧憬。在面临挑战、遭受挫折和感到无望之时，这本书会给您无穷的力量；在惶惑、痛苦和失落之际，这本书会给您以慰藉。相信它会成为您的终生益友，源源不断地为您生活的方方面面提供深沉的理解和智慧。

本书适合于大学一、二年级学生及同级英语水平的社会各界读者。在本书的编写过程中，郑玉萍付出了辛勤劳动，她反复阅读译文，并认真推敲了每一条注释，编者在此深表感谢。由于编者水平有限，疏漏之处难免，敬请各位读者指正。

编者

2008年1月

目　　录

"追求卓越"学英语丛书（英汉对照）

无尽的回味

——人生哲理美文精选

Endless Reflection: Elegant Writings on Life and Philosophy

◎ 谢艳明 编译

河南大学出版社
HENAN UNIVERSITY PRESS

图书在版编目(CIP)数据

无尽的回味:人生哲理美文精选:英汉对照/谢艳明编译.
2版(修订本)—开封:河南大学出版社,2008.4(2014.1重印)
(“追求卓越”学英语丛书)
ISBN 978-7-81091-766-7

Ⅰ.无… Ⅱ.谢… Ⅲ.①英语—汉语—对照读物②散文—作品集—世界 Ⅳ.H319.4:I

中国版本图书馆CIP数据核字(2008)第013894号

责任编辑 薛巧玲
责任校对 晓 雪
封面设计 今日文教

出 版	河南大学出版社		
	地址:河南省开封市明伦街85号	邮编:475001	
	电话:0378—2825001(营销部)	网址:www.hupress.com	
排 版	河南新华印刷集团有限公司		
印 刷	开封智圣印务有限公司		
版 次	2011年3月第2版	**印 次**	2014年1月第5次印刷
开 本	787mm×1092mm 1/16	**印 张**	13.25
字 数	224千字	**定 价**	24.00元

1. The Secret of True Happiness

I live in the land of Disney, Hollywood and year-round sun. You may think that people in such a glamorous① fun-filled place are happier than others. If so, you have some mistaken ideas about the nature of happiness.

Many intelligent② people equate happiness with fun. The truth is that fun and happiness have little or nothing in common. Fun is what we experience during the act. Happiness is what we experience after an act. It is deeper, more abiding emotion.

Going to an amusement park or ballgame, watching a movie or television, are fun activities that help us relax, temporarily③ forget our problems, and maybe even laugh. But, they do not bring happiness, because their positive effects end when the fun ends.

The way people cling to the belief that a fun-filled, pain-free life equals happiness, actually diminishes④ their chances of ever attaining⑤ real happiness. If fun and pleasure are equated with happiness, then pain must be equated with unhappiness. But, in fact, the opposite is true: more times than not, things that lead to happiness involve some pain.

As a result, many people avoid the very endeavors that are the source of true happiness. They fear the pain inevitably brought by such things as marriage, raising children, professional achievement, religious commitment⑥, civil or charitable work, self-improvement.

Ask a bachelor why he resists marriage even though he finds dating to be less and less satisfying. If he's honest, he will tell you that he is afraid of making a commitment. For commitment is in fact quite painful.

① glamorous['glæmərəs] *adj.* 富有魅力的,迷人的
② intelligent[in'telidʒənt] *adj.* 聪明的,伶俐的,有才智的
③ temporarily['tempərərili] *adv.* 临时地
④ diminish[di'miniʃ] *v.* (使)减少,(使)变小
⑤ attain[ə'tein] *vt.* 达到,获得
⑥ commitment[kə'mitmənt] *n.* 委托事项,许诺,承担义务

The single life is filled with fun, adventure, excitement. Marriage has such movement, but they are not its most distinguishing[1] features.

Similarly, couples who choose not to have children are deciding in favor of painless fun over painful happiness. They can dine out whenever they want, travel wherever they want and sleep as late as they want. Couples with infant children are lucky to get a whole night's sleep or a three-day vacation. I don't know any parent who would choose the word fun to describe raising children.

But couples who decide not to have children never experience the pleasure of hugging them or tucking them into bed at night. They never know the joys of watching a child grow up or of playing with a grandchild.

Of course I enjoy doing fun things. I like to play racquetball[2], joke with kids (and anybody else), and I probably have too many hobbies.

But these forms of fun do not contribute in any real way to my happiness. More difficult endeavors—writing, raising children, creating a deep relationship with my wife, trying to do good in the world—will bring me more happiness than what can ever be found in fun, that least permanent[3] of things.

Understanding and accepting that true happiness has nothing to do with fun is one of the most liberating realizations we can ever come to. It liberates time: Now we can devote more hours to activities that can genuinely[4] increase our happiness. It liberates money: Buying that new car or those fancy clothes that will do nothing to increase our happiness now seems pointless. And it liberates us from envy: We now understand that all those rich and glamorous people we were so

① distinguishing[dis'tiŋgwiʃiŋ] *adj.* 最明显的

② racquetball['rækitbɔːl] *n.* [体]壁球

③ permanent['pəːmənənt] *adj.* 永久的，持久的

④ genuinely['dʒenjuinli] *adv.* 真诚地，诚实地

sure are happy because they are always having so much fun actually may not be happy at all.

The moment we understand that fun does not bring happiness, we begin to lead our lives differently. The effect can be, quite literally, life-transforming.

真正幸福的秘密

我居住在迪斯尼乐园、好莱坞和终年阳光灿烂的地方。你或许认为生活在这种迷人的欢乐之乡的人们会比别人幸福。如果这么想,你就误解了幸福的本质。

很多聪明人都把幸福和快活混为一谈。其实,幸福和快活几乎没有共同点。快活是我们行为过程中的感受;幸福则是我们在行为完成后感觉到的,它比快活更深刻、更持久。

逛游乐园、参加球赛、观看电影或电视,这些都是令人感到快活的活动。它们能帮助我们放松,暂且忘掉一切问题,甚至使我们开怀大笑,但它们不能带来幸福,因为活动结束时,它们的积极效果也随之结束了。

一些人坚持认为充满乐趣、没有痛苦的生活就是幸福的生活,这种想法事实上使他们失去了获得真正幸福的机会。如果快活和高兴意味着幸福,那么痛苦肯定意味着不幸福。但事实与之相反:很多时候,幸福伴随着痛苦。

因此,很多人因为害怕痛苦而放弃了可能带来真正幸福的努力。婚姻、养育儿女、事业成功、宗教信仰、公益或慈善工作、自我提高等难免会带来痛苦,而他们害怕痛苦。

问一问单身汉,为什么他虽然越来越难满足于约会但仍然抵制结婚的诱惑。如果他是诚实的,他会告诉你,因为他害怕做出承诺。承诺事实上是非常痛苦的事,而单身生活充满有趣、冒险和刺激的事。婚姻也有这种令人高兴的事,但这不是其最明显的特征。

同样,选择不要孩子的夫妇宁可要没有痛苦的快活,也不要伴有痛苦的幸福。他们可以随时出去吃饭,想到哪儿旅游就到哪儿旅游,想多晚睡就多晚睡。而有幼儿的父母晚上能睡个囫囵觉或出门玩 3 天就算幸运了。我不知道哪对父母会用“快活”这个词来形容抚养孩子的经历。

但决定不要孩子的父母永远不可能体会到拥抱孩子或夜晚为孩子掖被

子时的愉悦心情。他们也永远无法体会到看着孩子成长或与孙辈玩耍时的幸福。

当然,我喜欢做快活的事。我喜欢玩壁球,喜欢和孩子们(也和别人)开玩笑。我的兴趣可能太广泛了。

但这些形式的娱乐并不能把我带向真正的幸福。一些更艰苦的事——写作、抚养孩子、和妻子建立深厚感情、在世上行善等等——会给我带来更大的幸福,是在快活中无法找到的幸福,而快活是最不能持久的感觉。

理解并承认幸福与快活无关是我们所能达到的最深刻的认识之一。它解放了时间:现在我们能把更多的时间投入到能真正给我们带来幸福的活动中。它解放了金钱:买那些无益于我们幸福的新车和新衣服现在显得毫无意义。这也把我们从嫉妒中解放出来:我们原以为那些富有、充满魅力的人们生活肯定幸福,因为他们有那么多有趣的活动,但现在我们理解,可能他们压根一点都不幸福。

一旦我们明白快活不能带来幸福,我们就会开始过一种不同的生活。这可能才是脱胎换骨。

2. Love Is a Telephone

Love is a telephone which always keeps silent when you are longing for a call, but rings when you are not ready for it. As a result, we often miss the sweetness from the other end.

Love is a telephone which is seldom program-controlled or directly dialed. You cannot get an immediate answer by a mere "hello", let alone go deep into your lover's heart by one call. Usually it has to be relayed① by an operator, and you have to be patient② in waiting. Destiny is the operator of this phone, who is always irresponsible③ and fond of laying practical jokes to which she may make you a lifelong victim intentionally④ or unintentionally.

Love is a telephone which is always busy. When you are ready to die for love, you only find, to your disappointment, the line is already occupied by⑤ someone else, and you are greeted only by a busy line. This is an eternal⑥ regret handed down from generation to generation and you are only one of those who languish for⑦ followers.

Love is a telephone which is sometimes so sensitive that you are put through by a single dial and responded to as soon as you say "hello". But, more often than not, you only hang it up and turn away sadly just because of its lack of challenge and effort. Once you realize your mistake, no one is available at the

① relay[riː'lei] *v.* 传递,使接替,转播
② patient['peiʃənt] *adj.* 忍耐的,耐心的
③ irresponsible[ˌiris'pɔnsəbl] *adj.* 不负责任的,不可靠的
④ intentionally[in'tenʃənəli] *adv.* 有意地,故意地
⑤ be occupied by *vt.* 被占据
⑥ eternal[i(ː)'təːnl] *adj.* 永恒的,永远的
⑦ languish for *v.* 因渴望而苦恼

other end.

Love is a telephone, but it is difficult to seize the center time for dialing, and you will let slip the opportunity if your call is either too early or too late.

Love is a telephone which is not always associated with happiness. Honeyed words are transmitted by sound waves, but when the lovers are brought together, the phone serves no purpose that many lovers observe that marriage is the doom of love.

Love is a telephone which, when you use it for the first time, makes you so nervous and excited that you either hold the receiver① upside down or dial the wrong number. By the time you've calmed down, you will beat a loss to whom you should make the call.

Love is a telephone which often has crossed lines. And this usually happens to you unexpectedly. Your time will either cross or be crossed. Both cases are referred to as "triangle". Fortunately, all such occurrences are transient. ②

爱情是一部电话

爱情是一部电话，在你渴望它响起时，它却总是默无声息；在你没有为之准备时，它却丁零作响。因此，我们常常错过电话那头传来的甜蜜。

爱情这部电话很少是程控或直拨的。你不可能仅凭一声"喂"就马上得到回音，更不要说呼唤一声就走进爱人的心。它通常必须有接线员转接，你得耐心等待。命运就是这部电话的接线员，她总是不负责任，喜欢搞恶作剧。她也许有意无意地使你成为终生的牺牲品。

爱情是一部总是忙碌的电话。当你准备为爱献身时，令你失望的是，你却发现电话已经占线，迎接你的只是忙音。这是人类代代相袭的永恒的遗

① receiver[ri'siːvə] *n.* 听筒

② transient['trænziənt] *adj.* 短暂的，瞬时的

憾，只不过你是那众多为爱而烦恼的追随者之一。

爱情是一部有时非常灵敏的电话，一拨即通，一“喂”即应。可是，你常常只是因为它缺乏挑战、不费气力而挂机，伤心地转身离去。一旦你认识到自己的错误，另一端却无人接听。

爱情是一部电话，但很难抓准拨号时机。无论拨得太早还是拨得太晚，你都会错失良机。

爱情是一部电话，它并不总是和幸福息息相关。尽管甜言蜜语由声波传送，但当相爱的人生活在一起时，电话发挥不了作用。难怪许多相爱的人说婚姻是爱情的坟墓。

爱情是一部电话，你第一次使用时，它会让你感到紧张激动，不是拿倒了话筒，就是拨错了号码。等你平静下来时，却常常不知道该给谁打电话。

爱情是一部电话，它经常串线，而且串线常常是在你意想不到的时候发生的。不是你的电话与别人的串线，就是别人的电话与你的串线。这两种情况都被称为“三角恋爱”。幸运的是，所有这些串线都是很短暂的。

3. The Five Images of Love

No one understands the nature of love; it is like a bird of heaven that sings a strange language. It lights down among us, coming from whence we know not, going we know not how or when, striking out wild notes of music that make even fatigued and heavy hearts to throb and give back a tone of courage.

The sorts and kinds of love are infinite① in number, infinite as the days of the years of time. Each one of us is capable of many and various loves. We cannot love two creatures, not two dogs, with the same love. To each of those whom we love we offer a gem of different color and value; to the unknown Master of the heavens, ah! who shall tell of what sort is the love we offer to Him? Yet in this love, too (which is natural worship), we discover the same vibrational② atmosphere that invades the soul of all lovers.

I doubt we shall not get much nearer to the nature of love by mere talking. Intellectual statements are of little use. God does not make intellectual statements, He creates. We have to find our way about in the vast medley③ of created things that life spreads out around us, and pick up what bits of knowledge we can as we make our way along.

Let me choose five images that will give an idea of what the awaking of this new life means.

Ⅰ. Shall we not say that the creature without love is

① infinite['infinit] *adj.* 无穷的，无限的，无数的，极大的

② vibrational[vai'breiʃənəl] *adj.* 振动的，摇摆的

③ medley['medli] *n.* 杂乱的一团，混杂的人群

like the lamp unlit? There it is, and no one needs it. But touch it with flame, and it trembles and glows and becomes the centre of the room where it stands. Everything that falls under its rays is new-gilt. So does the lover see all natural things quite new.

Ⅱ. Or take the image of the withering plant that is dying of drought. The sun's rays have parched it; the roots have searched and searched for moisture① in a soil that grows every day harder and drier. The plant wilts and hangs its head; it is fainting and ready to die, when down comes the rain in a murmuring multitude② of round scented③ drops. The purest thing alive, a distilled④ essence, necessary to life. Under that baptism⑤ the plant lifts itself up; it drinks and rejoices. In the night it renews its strength; in the morning the heat it has had from the sun, reinforced by the rain, bursts out into colored flowers. So I have known a man battered by hard life and the excess of his own passions: I have seen love come to such a man and take him up and cleanse him and set him on his feet; and from him has burst forth a flood of color and splendor⑥—creative work that now lends its fiery stimulus to thousands.

Ⅲ. Another image might be of the harp that stands by itself in golden aloofness⑦. Then come the beautiful arms, the curving fingers that pluck at the strings, and the air is filled with melody⑧; the harp begins to live, thrilling and rejoicing, down to its golden foot.

Ⅳ. Or picture the unlighted house, empty at fall of night. The windows are dark; the door shut; the clean wind goes about and about it, and cannot find an entrance. The dull heavy air is faint within; it longs to be reunited to the wind of the world outside. Then comes the woman

① moisture[ˈmɔistʃə] *n.* 潮湿,湿气
② multitude[ˈmʌltitjuːd] *n.* 多数,群众
③ scented[ˈsentid] *adj.* 洒有香水的,有香味的
④ distilled[disˈtild] *adj.* 由蒸馏得来的
⑤ baptism[ˈbæptizəm] *n.* 浸洗,洗礼
⑥ splendor[ˈsplendə] *n.* 光彩,壮观,杰出
⑦ aloofness[əˈluːfnis] *n.* 超然态度
⑧ melody[ˈmelədi] *n.* 悦耳的音调

with the key, and in she steps; the windows are opened, the imprisoned air rushes out, the wind enters; the lamps and the fire are lit; so that light fills windows and doors. The tables are set, there is the sound of footsteps; and more footsteps. The house glows and lives.

One could please oneself by many more images; such as the white garment① of feathers that the young swans put on in the spring: the young flowers opening out their cups to the Sun that fills them with his golden wine. All life is full of such images, because nature has ruled that love, energy, beauty, and joy are one.

Ⅴ. A last image only I would like to add because of the pleasure it has given me. On the north door of the Cathedral of Charters there is a sculptured② design, some six hundred years old, of God creating the birds. God is charming, quite young, not more than thirty-eight or so; He has a most sweet expression. Behind Him a little stands the Son, about seventeen, tall as He and very like Him, but beardless. He has the same sweetness of look, as though upon each countenance③ an ineffable④ smile were just dawning. The Father is holding something that time has broken in His hand; most likely it is a bird.

What a fortunate moment! What a fortunate thought! No wonder they both look pleased. Never have the birds disappointed Him as have we, His ruder children. Every spring since then these small creatures praise Him, head turned skywards, for the joy of the beloved, for the secret nest.

Imagining and pondering, one is apt to grow a little wise ; now perhaps we may

① garment[ˈgɑːmənt] n. 衣服，外衣，外表

② sculpture[ˈskʌlptʃə] v. 雕刻

③ countenance[ˈkauntinəns] n. 面容，脸色

④ ineffable[inˈefəbl] adj. 不能说的，不应说出的，避讳的

say that love is a radiant① atmosphere of the soul, a celestial② energy, a fluid force.

This force, this energy is set running in the wide kingdom that is within us by some spirit touch. A soft tumult③ takes place in the life within; waves on waves of joy, desire, grief, ecstasy④ begin to run, making a trembling music that often causes the whole body to shake and tremble too.

I am in love with love; I do adore it;—from the smile on that rough fellow's face as he talks to his dog, to the ardors of a St. Francis or a Joan of Arc. That bright creative flame, winged, conferring⑤ the gift of tongues, master of all music, of all joy, is the best thing we have of life.

五个爱的意象

没有人理解爱的本质,它就像天堂里的鸟,吟唱着陌生的语言。它的光辉普照我们,它来无影,去无踪,它敲击出狂野的音乐,使疲惫、沉重的心灵为之跳动,呼唤出勇敢的乐音。

爱之多样,数不胜数,如年年月月、时时刻刻。我们每个人都具有各种不同的爱之能力,我们不会以同一种方式去爱恋两个人、两条狗。对每一位我们钟爱的人,我们奉献的是色彩不同、价值各异的宝石。对天国神秘的主,谁能说清我们奉献的是什么样的爱? 然而,在这爱恋(这自然崇拜)之中,我们发现,侵入所有爱者心灵的,是相同的震颤。

我不信我们的讨论探讨不出爱之真谛。理性陈述常苍白无力,上帝不作理性陈述,上帝创造! 我们要在生活展现给我们的无数繁杂的创造物之中,找到自己的方式,并在前行的过程中收集一点一滴的知识。

我选择五个意象来描画这一新生活之复苏意味着什么。

① radiant[ˈreidjənt] *adj.* 发光的,辐射的,容光焕发的
② celestial[siˈlestʃəl] *adj.* 天空的;神圣的
③ tumult[ˈtjuːmʌlt] *n.* 吵闹,骚动,拥挤,混乱
④ ecstasy[ˈekstəsi] *n.* 入迷
⑤ confer[kənˈfəː] *v.* 授予

首先，我们难道不能说无爱的生灵就如未点燃的灯吗？它在那里，却没人需要。点上火苗，它摇曳，闪光，成了屋子的中心。在它的照耀下，一切都似乎重新镀了一层金。所以在拥有爱的人的眼里，世界全是新的。

其次，没有爱就像即将死于干旱的枯萎植物。太阳的光烧烤着它，植物的根在日益坚硬干枯的土壤里寻觅水分。植物枯萎了，耷拉下脑袋。就在它晕眩之际、快要死去之时，突然下起酣畅的、圆圆的、芬芳的雨滴，那是生命的甘霖。在雨水的洗礼之下，植物昂起了头，它畅饮，它欢欣。夜晚，它恢复了体力。白天，它享受雨后强劲的阳光，绽放出五彩之花。我认识一位被艰难的生活和自己过度情感打磨的男人，我看到爱普降于他，扶持他，净化他，并支撑着他站立起来，使之迸发出壮丽与光彩——现在成了激励无数人的创新杰作。

第三，另一个意象是一尊超然独立的竖琴，拨动琴弦的美丽手臂和纤纤玉指，让空气中弥漫起悦耳的旋律。竖琴顿时活了，开始振奋和欢欣，其情绪一直感染至琴基。

第四，没有爱就像秋夜中一栋没有光亮的空房，窗口黑暗，大门紧闭，清新的风儿绕着它无法吹进。屋内沉闷的空气让人昏厥，渴望与外面清新的风儿汇集。这时，一位手持钥匙的佳人翩然而至，步入室内，推开窗，囚禁的空气狂涌而出，清风穿进；点亮灯，点燃炉，灯火照亮门窗。餐桌摆放停当，脚步声接踵而来，屋子开始弥漫起活力与生机。

人们可以想象出更多自己喜欢的画面，比如春天里小天鹅生长起的洁白羽毛；向着给自己注入金色琼浆的太阳开放的花蕾。所有的生命都充满了这样的意象，因为大自然裁定：爱、活力、美和愉悦浑然合一。

第五，我要补充的最后一个意象，是因为它曾经给我带来愉悦。沙特尔大教堂北门上的一个雕刻设计，有大约 600 年之久，上面雕的是上帝造鸟。上帝很迷人，很年轻，大概 38 岁左右，他表情甜美，身后站着天子，大约 17 岁，和他一般高，跟他很相像，但没有胡子。他的脸上泛着同样甜美的神情，好像所有的表情中都呈现出一种不可言喻的微笑。天父正握着时间开辟于他手中的东西，很可能是一只鸟。

多么幸运的时刻！多么吉利的主意！难怪他们看上去都很高兴。鸟儿从未像我们，他粗鲁的孩子一样，让他失望。从那以后，每到春天，这些小生灵便仰望长空，为心爱人儿的愉悦、为隐秘的鸟巢而赞美他。

想象与沉思，它能让我们变得更为明智。现在我们也许会说，爱是灵魂璀璨的氛围，是精妙的活力，是流动的力量。

这力量，这活力被某种精神触觉所导引，在我们宽广的身体王国中奔跑。生活中，温软的骚动被拨动，愉悦、欲望、悲伤和狂喜开始交替涌起，奏起让全身心震颤的乐音。

我与爱相恋，我真的很爱慕它——从那粗汉与自己的狗儿聊天时脸上呈现的微笑之中，从他对某个圣弗兰西斯或圣女贞德的热忱之中。那光亮创新的火焰，圣灵所赐的口才，所有音乐、愉悦的主人，是我们从生活中获取的最佳赏赐。

4. Hungry for Your Love

It is cold, so bitter cold, on this dark, winter day in 1942. But it is no different from any other day in this Nazi concentration camp. I stand shivering in my thin rags, still in disbelief that this nightmare is happening. I am just a young boy. I should be playing with friends; I should be going to school; I should be looking forward to a future, to growing up and marrying, and having a family of my own. But those dreams are for the living, and I am no longer one of them. Instead, I am almost dead, surviving from day to day, from hour to hour, ever since I was taken from my home and brought here with tens of thousands other Jews. Will I still be alive tomorrow? Will I be taken to the gas chamber tonight?

Back and forth I walk next to the barbed① wire fence, trying to keep my emaciated② body warm. I am hungry, but I have been hungry for longer than I want to remember. I am always hungry. Edible③ food seems like a dream. Each day as more of us disappear, the happy past seems like a mere dream, and I sink deeper and deeper into despair. Suddenly, I notice a young girl walking past on the other side of the barbed wire. She stops and looks at me with sad eyes, eyes that seem to say that she understands, that she, too, cannot fathom④ why I am here. I want to look away, oddly ashamed for this stranger to see me like this, but I cannot tear my eyes from hers.

Then she reaches into her pocket, and pulls out a red apple. A beautiful, shiny red apple. Oh, how long has it been since I have seen one! She looks cautiously to the left and to the right, and then with a

① barbed[bɑːbd] *adj.* 有刺的，有倒钩的

② emaciated[iˈmeiʃieitid] *adj.* 瘦弱的，衰弱的

③ edible[ˈedibl] *adj.* 可食用的

④ fathom[ˈfæðəm] *v.* 看穿，彻底了解

smile of triumph①, quickly throws the apple over the fence. I run to pick it up, holding it in my trembling, frozen fingers. In my world of death, this apple is an expression of life, of love. I glance up in time to see the girl disappearing into the distance.

The next day, I cannot help myself—I am drawn at the same time to that spot near the fence. Am I crazy for hoping she will come again? Of course. But in here, I cling to② any tiny scrap of hope. She has given me hope and I must hold tightly to it.

And again, she comes. And again, she brings me an apple, flinging it over the fence with that same sweet smile.

This time I catch it, and hold it up for her to see. Her eyes twinkle. Does she pity me? Perhaps. I do not care, though. I am just so happy to gaze at her. And for the first time in so long, I feel my heart move with emotion.

For seven months, we meet like this. Sometimes we exchange a few words. Sometimes, just an apple. But she is feeding more than my belly, this angel from heaven. She is feeding my soul. And somehow, I know I am feeding hers as well.

One day, I hear frightening news: we are being shipped to another camp. This could mean the end for me. And it definitely means the end for me and my friend.

The next day when I greet her, my heart is breaking, and I can barely speak as I say what must be said: "Do not bring me an apple tomorrow," I tell her. "I am being sent to another camp. We will never see each other again." Turning before I lose all control, I run away from the fence. I cannot bear to look back. If I did, I know she would see me standing there, with tears streaming down my face.

Months pass and the nightmare③ continues. But the memory of this

① triumph['traiəmf] n. 胜利,成功
② cling to 依附,依靠,坚持
③ nightmare['naitmeə] n. 梦魇,噩梦,可怕的事物

girl sustains① me through the terror, the pain, the hopelessness. Over and over in my mind, I see her face, her kind eyes, I hear her gentle words, I taste those apples.

And then one day, just like that, the nightmare is over. The war has ended. Those of us who are still alive are freed. I have lost everything that was precious to me, including my family. But I still have the memory of this girl, a memory I carry in my heart and a memory that gives me the will to go on as I move to America to start a new life.

Years pass. It is 1957. I am living in New York City. A friend convinces me to go on a blind date with a lady friend of his. Reluctantly②, I agree. But she is nice, this woman named Roma. And like me, she is an immigrant③, so we have at least that in common.

"Where were you during the war?" Roma asks me gently, in that delicate④ way immigrants ask one another questions those years.

"I was in a concentration camp in Germany," I reply.

Roma gets a far away look in her eyes, as if she is remembering something painful yet sweet.

"What is it?" I ask.

"I am just thinking something from my past, Herman," Roma explains in a voice suddenly very soft. "You see, when I was a young girl, I lived near a concentration camp. There was a boy there, a prisoner, and for a long while, I used to visit him every day. I remember I used to bring him apples. I would throw the apple over the fence, and he would be so happy."

Roma sighs heavily and continues. "It is hard to describe how we felt

---

① sustain[səs'tein] *v.* 支撑，撑住

② reluctantly[ri'lʌktəntli] *adv.* 不情愿地，不愿意地

③ immigrant['imigrənt] *n.* 移民，侨民

④ delicate['delikit] *adj.* 精巧的，精致的，病弱的，脆弱的，微妙的

each other—after all, we were young, and we only exchanged a few words when we could—but I can tell you, there was much love there. I assume① he was killed like so many others. But I cannot bear to think that, and so I try to remember him as he was for those months we were given together."

With my heart pounding so loudly I think it will explode②, I look directly at Roma and ask, "And did that boy say to you one day, 'Do not bring me an apple tomorrow. I am being sent to another camp?'"

"Why, yes," Roma responds, her voice trembling.

"But, Herman, how on earth could you possibly know that?"

I take her hands in mine and answer, "Because I was that young boy, Roma."

For many moments, there is only silence. We cannot take our eyes from each other, and as the veils of time lift, we recognize the soul behind the eyes, the dear friend we once loved so much, whom we have never stopped loving, whom we have never stopped remembering.

Finally, I speak: "Look, Roma, I was separated from you once, and I don't ever want to be separated from you again. Now, I am free, and I want to be together with you forever. Dear, will you marry me?"

I see that same twinkle in her eyes that I used to see as Roma says, "Yes, I will marry you," and we embrace, the embrace we longed to share for so many months, but barbed wire came between us. Now, nothing ever will again.

Almost forty years have passed since that day when I found my Roma again. Destiny brought us together the first time during the war to show me a promise of hope and now it had reunited us to fulfill that promise.

Valentine's Day, 1996. I bring Roma to the Oprah Winfrey Show to honor her on national television. I want to tell her in front of millions of people what I feel in my heart every day:

---

① assume[ə'sjuːm] *v.* 假定,设想

② explode[iks'pləud] *vi.* 爆炸,爆发,激发

"Darling, you fed me in the concentration camp when I was hungry. And I am still hungry, for something I will never get enough of: I am only hungry for your love."

渴望你的爱

那是1942年的一个阴暗潮湿、寒冷刺骨的冬日。在这个纳粹集中营中，这一天和往日并没有什么不同。我衣衫褴褛、瑟瑟发抖地站在那里，仍然怀疑这个正在发生的可怕的梦魇。我只是个小男孩，此时的我，本应该和朋友们一起玩耍；本应该去学堂读书；本应该期待一个未来，期待长大成人后结婚生子，期待拥有一个属于自己的家。而这些只是那些活着的人的梦想，我已经不是他们之中的一员。实际上，自从我从家中和成千上万的犹太人被带到这里之后，我几乎接近死亡，只是日复一日、时时刻刻苟延残喘。我明天会不会依然能够存活？今晚我会不会被带到毒气室？

在靠近那个铁丝网栅栏的地方，我来来回回地徜徉，以期能够让我那瘦弱不堪的身体暖和一点点。我非常饥饿，而我已经记不得这种饥饿感持续了多久。我一直很饿，能吃的食物对我来说就像一个梦。每天，随着越来越多的人消失，过去的快乐时光恍若一梦，而我也越来越深地陷入了绝望。突然，我看到有一位少女从铁丝栅栏的对面走过。她停下脚步，用哀伤的眼睛望着我，那双眼睛似乎在说她理解我，似乎也在说不理解我为什么站在那里。被一个陌生人这样看着，我感到莫名的羞耻，想把脸转过去，可是我的泪水却止不住地淌下来。

然后，她将手伸进自己的口袋，把一个红苹果拿了出来。一个美丽诱人、闪闪发亮的红苹果。哇，我好久没有见过这样的苹果了！她小心翼翼地向左看了看，又向右看了看，然后脸上挂着一丝胜利的笑容，迅速地将苹果扔过栅栏。我跑过去将苹果捡了起来，用我冰冷、颤抖的双手紧紧地握着它。在这个处处充斥着死亡的世界里，这个红苹果就是生命的释然，爱的表达。我抬起头来，却看到那位少女消失在远处。

第二天，迫不及待的我，在同一时间

又来到了靠近栅栏的那个地方。我渴望她再次到来吗？确实如此，在这里，我紧紧抓住任何一丝微渺的希望。她给了我希望，我必须紧紧抓住它。

再一次，她来了。再一次，她给我带来一个苹果，带着同样甜蜜的微笑，她将苹果扔过栅栏。

这次我接住了苹果，举起来让她看了看。她眨了眨眼睛。她是同情我吗？可能吧。我不关心这些，我只是很高兴能看到她。许久以来，我的心第一次被深深地感动。

7 个月来，我们一直用这种方式见面。有时候我们会交谈几句，有时候，仅仅用一个苹果而已。然而，这个来自天堂的天使，不仅仅是喂饱了我的肚子，更充实了我的灵魂。从某种程度上说，我也充实了她的灵魂。

一天，我听到了一个可怕的消息：我们要被运送到另外一个集中营。这意味着我的一切结束了，更意味着我和我的朋友也结束了。

第二天见到她时，我听到我的心破裂的声音，我几乎无法表达我必须说的话语："明天不要带苹果给我了，"我告诉她。"我要被送往另外一个集中营。我们再也无法相见了。"转身之前我已经控制不住自己，跑离栅栏而去。我不忍心向后看，如果看了，会让她看到我站在那里，泪流满面。

几个月过去，噩梦在继续。对这位少女的记忆一直支撑着我度过那些充满恐惧、痛苦和绝望的日子。在我的脑海里，我一次又一次地看到她的脸庞，她那充满温暖的眼睛，我听到她温柔的话语，品尝到那些美味的苹果。

就在噩梦结束的那一天，战争也结束了。我们那些存活下来的人也获取了自由。我失去了对我重要的一切，包括我的家庭。然而，对这位少女的记忆一直在我的脑海里，后来我移居到美国开始新的生活，这份记忆一直流淌在我的心底，给了我继续生存的勇气。

多年过去，那是 1957 年，我住在纽约的时候。在一位朋友的劝说下，我勉强答应了去和他的一位女性朋友初次约会。她是一位叫罗玛的美丽女子，和我一样，也是移民。至少我们还有共同点。

"战争期间你在哪里?"罗玛温柔地问我，在那个年代，这是移民相互询问彼此情况的微妙方式。

"我在德国的一个集中营，"我回答说。

罗玛的眼神若有所思，似乎她正在回忆一些痛苦而又甜蜜的事。

"你在想什么?"我问。

"我正在回忆我过去的事，赫尔曼。"罗玛突然用特别温柔的声音解释说。"在我还是少女的时候，我住在一个集中营附近。那里有个男孩，是个战俘，很长一段时间，我每天都去看望他。我还记得我带苹果给他。我记得我每次把苹果扔过栅栏，他就会很快乐。”

罗玛深深地叹息了一声，继续说：“很难形容我们是如何感受彼此的，当时我们毕竟还小，只有在可能的情况下交谈几句话——可是，我可以告诉你，我们之间确实有爱。我想他像许多其他人一样被杀害了。可是我却无法容忍自己想到这些，所以我努力去想我们曾经在一起的那几个月中他的模样。”

我的心怦怦跳得几乎要爆炸了，我直直地盯着罗玛说：“那个男孩有一天是不是告诉你，‘明天不要再带苹果给我了，我要被送往另一个集中营’？”

“是的，你怎么？”罗玛回应说，声音在颤抖。

“可是，赫尔曼，你怎么会知道这些呢？”

我一下抓住她的手，告诉她说：“因为我就是那位男孩，罗玛。”

许久许久，只是沉默。我们无法将眼睛从彼此身上移开，时间的面纱揭去了，我们认出隐藏在眼睛下面的灵魂，我们曾经彼此深爱过的挚友，我们从来没有停止爱过，从来没有停止想念的挚友。

最后我说：“瞧，罗玛，我曾经和你分开过，不想再次和你分开了。现在我自由了，我想永远和你在一起。亲爱的，嫁给我好吗？”

如同往日见过的眼神，我看到她的眼睛眨了眨，说：“嗯，我愿意嫁给你。”说完我们拥抱彼此，这是诸多时日以来我们所渴望的、却被铁丝网挡住的拥抱。现在，我们之间没有任何障碍。

自从我再次找到我的罗玛，40 个年头已经过去。在战争期间，命运让我们第一次相聚，让我看到了希望的承诺；现在，命运再次让我们相聚，只是为了实现那份曾经的承诺。

1996 年的情人节，我带罗玛去参加了奥普拉 · 温菲利脱口秀节目。我想在千万万人面前告诉罗玛我每天的感受：

“亲爱的，在我饥饿的时候，你在集中营里喂饱了我。我仍然饥饿，渴望得到那些对我来说永远不够多的：我渴望得到你的爱。”

5. A Simple Truth About Happiness

After I gave a talk on the subject of happiness, a woman in the audience stood up and said, "I wish my husband had come." "Much as I loved him," she explained, "it wasn't easy being married to someone so unhappy." This woman enabled me to put into words what I had been searching for—altruistic①, as well as the personal reasons for taking happiness seriously. I told her that each of us owes it to our spouse②, our children, and our friends to be as happy as we can.

I was not a particularly happy child, and like most teenagers, I took pleasure in my anguish③. One day, however, it occurred to me that I was taking the easy way out. Anyone could be unhappy; it took no courage and effort. True achievement lay in struggling to be happy. The notion that we have to work at happiness comes as news to many people. We assume it's a feeling that comes as a result of good things that just happen to us, things over which we have little or no control. But the opposite is true: happiness is largely under our control. It is a battle to be fought and not a feeling to be awaited. To achieve a happy life, it's necessary to overcome some stumbling blocks④, three of which are:

Comparison with Others. Most of us compare ourselves with anyone we think is happier—a relative, an acquaintance⑤ or, often someone we barely know. I once met a young man who struck me as particularly successful and happy. He spoke of his love for his beautiful wife and their three daughters, and of his joy at being a radio talk-show host in a city he loved. I remember thinking that he was one of those lucky few for whom everything goes effortlessly right. Then we started talking about the

① altruistic[ˌæltru'istik] *adj.* 利他的,无私心的
② spouse[spauz] *n.* 配偶
③ anguish['æŋɡwiʃ] *n.* 极度的痛苦,苦恼
④ stumbling blocks *n.* 障碍物,绊脚石
⑤ acquaintance[ə'kweintəns] *n.* 相识,熟人

Internet. He blessed its existence, he told me, because he could look up information on multiple sclerosis① — the terrible disease afflicting② his wife. I felt like a fool for assuming nothing unhappy existed in his life.

Images of Perfection. Almost all of us have images of how life should be. The problem, of course, is that only rarely do people's jobs, spouses and children live up to these imagined ideals. Here's a personal example: no one in my family had ever divorced. I assumed that marriage was for life. So when my wife and I divorced after five years of marriage and three years after the birth of our son, my world collapsed. I was a failure in my own eyes. I later remarried and confided③ to my wife that I couldn't shake the feeling that my family life had failed. She asked me what was wrong with our family now (which included her daughter from a previous marriage and my son). I had to admit that, aside from the pain of being with my son only half the time (my ex-wife and I shared custody④), our family life was wonderful. "Then why don't you celebrate it?" she asked. That's what I decided to do. But first I had to get rid of a "perfect" family.

"Missing Tile" Syndrome⑤. One effective way of destroying happiness is to look at something and focus on even the smallest flaw. It's like looking at the tiled ceiling and concentrating on the space where one tile is missing. As a bald man told me, "whenever I enter a room, all I see is hair."

---

① sclerosis[skliə'rəusis]n. [医]硬化症，硬化，硬结
② afflict[ə'flikt]v. 使痛苦，折磨
③ confide[kən'faid]v. 倾诉，委托，信赖
④ custody['kʌstədi]n. 监管，监护权
⑤ syndrome['sindrəum]n. 综合病症

Once you've determined what your missing tile is, explore whether acquiring it will really make you happy. Then do one of the three things: get it, replace it with a different tile, or forget about it and focus on the tiles in your life that are not missing.

We all know people who have had a relatively easy life yet are essentially unhappy. And we know people who have suffered a great deal but generally remain happy. The first secret is gratitude①. All happy people are grateful. Ungrateful② people cannot be happy. We tend to think that being unhappy leads people to complain, but it's truer to say that complaining leads to people becoming unhappy.

The second secret is realizing that happiness is a byproduct of something else. The most obvious sources are those pursuits③ that give our lives purpose—anything from studying insects to playing baseball. The more passions we have, the more happiness we are likely to experience. Finally, the belief that something permanent④ transcends us and that our existence has some larger meaning can help us be happier. We need a spiritual faith, or a philosophy of life. Whatever your philosophy, it should include this truism: if you choose to find the positive in virtually every situation, you will be blessed, and if you choose to find the awful, you will be cursed. As with happiness itself, this is largely your decision to make.

关于幸福的真谛

我做完一篇关于幸福的演讲之后，一位女听众站起来说："我希望我的丈夫也来听听。"她解释说，"尽管我很爱他，但嫁给一个性情如此不快乐的人不是一件容易的事情。"这位女子让我想起了我一直在寻找的词语——无私，以及严肃对待幸福的个人原因。我告诉她，多亏了这一点，我们每个人

① gratitude[ˈgrætitjuːd] *n.* 感激，感恩

② ungrateful[ʌnˈgreitful] *adj.* 不领情的

③ pursuits[pəˈsjuːts] *n.* 追击

④ permanent[ˈpəːmənənt] *adj.* 永久的，持久的

才能使得配偶、孩子和朋友像我们一样快乐幸福。

我并非一个特别快乐的孩子，像许多青少年一样，我独自享受着痛苦。然而，有一天，我想到一个摆脱这种苦恼的好办法。不需要鼓励也不需要费力，每个人都可以不快乐。真正的成功在于为幸福而努力。我们主张为幸福而努力却让许多人感到惊奇。我们认为这是一种发生在我们身上的一种美好的感情，这是我们不能控制的或者难以控制的事情。而实际情况是：在很大程度上，我们能够控制我们的幸福。这是一场为之奋斗的战争，而非一直静候的感情。为了拥有幸福的生活，我们有必要克服一些绊脚石，有三个绊脚石是这样的：

和其他人做比较。我们许多人喜欢拿自己和那些我们认为比自己要幸福的人做比较——一位亲戚，一个熟人，或者是我们刚刚认识的人。我曾经遇见一位年轻人，他的成功和快乐的形象深深打动了我。他对我讲起了他美丽的妻子、三个女儿，还有在自己喜欢的那个城市里做电台脱口秀主持人的工作。我记得他是那种少有的幸运儿，一切进展得特别顺利的人。然后我们又聊起了网络。他告诉我，他受益于因特网的存在，因为他可以从网上查询一些有关多种硬化症的信息——一种一直折磨他妻子的可怕的疾病。我觉得自己像个傻子，竟然想象他生活中没有一丝不幸的存在。

完美的形象。我们所有的人都想象过生活的原本模样。当然，问题在于很少有人在职业、配偶、孩子等方面做到这些想象中的完美形象。就拿我个人来说：我的家族中没有离婚的历史，我想，婚姻就是为了生活。于是，在我结婚5年之后，也就是我儿子3岁那年，我和我妻子离了婚，那时候我的世界都垮了。我个人认为我是失败的。后来，再婚后我对妻子说，我无法摆脱家庭生活失败的阴影。她就问我现在的家庭生活有什么问题（包括她上次婚姻中所生的女儿和我的儿子）。我承认说，除了我和我儿子只能有一半时间待在一起这种痛苦之外（我前妻和我对他都有监护权），我们的家庭生活是完美的。“那你为什么不庆祝一番呢？”她问。那正是我想做的。而首先，我必须摆脱“完美”家庭的困扰。

“缺失的瓦片”综合征。破坏幸福的一个有效方式就是，关注某件事情，并把重点放在最细小的瑕

疵上。正如当一个人注视着平坦的天花板时,却将注意力放在一个缺失的瓦片上面一样。就像一个秃顶的人告诉我说,“无论何时我走进房间,我看到的只是头发。”你一旦发现你缺失的瓦片是什么,就努力找出你是否在得到它之后会倍感幸福。那么就做这三件事情吧:找到它,并用不同的瓦片替代它,或者忘掉它,关注你生活中没有缺失的瓦片。

众所周知,拥有舒适生活的人基本上是不快乐的。而那些饱受人生苦难的人通常拥有快乐的性情。第一个秘诀就是保持一颗感恩的心。所有快乐幸福的人都是心怀感恩的,而那些不感恩的人往往不会快乐。我们都认为,不快乐的人往往容易抱怨,而更真实地说,抱怨往往会令人更加不快乐。

第二个秘诀就是,要意识到快乐是其他事情的附属物。显然,快乐的源泉来自那些赋予生活目标的追求——从研究昆虫到打棒球。我们拥有的激情越多,就越容易体验到快乐。最后,要有超越我们永恒的信念,要相信我们的存在在很大意义上让我们更加快乐。我们需要精神信仰,或者是处世哲学。无论你的处世哲学是什么,都应该有这种利他主义:在任何情形下,如果你选择去发现积极的一面,你就感受到幸福;如果你选择去发现糟糕的一面,你就会感到苦恼。至于快乐本身,很大程度上取决于你的决定。

6. Some Meanings of Authentic Love

Love means that I know the person I love. I'm aware of the many sides of the other person—not just the beautiful side but also the limitations, inconsistencies① and flaws.

Love means that I care about the welfare② of the person I love. If I care about you, I'm concerned about your growth, and I hope you will become all that you can become.

Love means having respect for the dignity③ of the person I love. If I love you, I can see you as a separate person, with your own values and thoughts and feelings, and I do not insist that you surrender your identity④ and conform⑤ to an image of what I expect you to be for me.

Love means having a responsibility toward the person I love. If I love you, I'm responsive to most of your major needs as a person.

Love means growth for both myself and the person I love. If I love you, I am growing as a result of my love. You are a stimulant⑥ for me to become more fully what I might become, and my loving enhances your being as well.

Love means making a commitment to the person I love. This commitment does not entail⑦ surrendering our total selves to each other; nor does it imply that the relationship is necessarily permanent. It does entail a willingness to stay with each other in times of pain, uncertainty, struggle, and despair, as well as in times of calm and enjoyment.

Love means trusting the person I love. If I love you, I trust that you will accept my caring and my love and that you won't deliberately hurt

---

① inconsistency[ˌinkənˈsistənsi] *n.* 不协调，矛盾

② welfare[ˈwelfɛə] *n.* 福利，安宁，幸福

③ dignity[ˈdigniti] *n.* 尊严，高贵

④ identity[aiˈdentiti] *n.* 身份

⑤ conform[kənˈfɔːm] *v.* 使遵守，使顺从，符合

⑥ stimulant[ˈstimjulənt] *n.* 刺激物

⑦ entail[inˈteil] *v.* 使必需，使蒙受，使承担，遗传给

me. I trust the reciprocal① nature of our love.

Love can tolerate② imperfection. In a love relationship there are times of boredom, times when I may feel like giving up, times of real strain, and times I experience an impasse③. Authentic④ love does not imply enduring happiness. I can stay during rough times, however, because I can remember what we had together in the past, and I can picture what we will have together in our future if we care enough to face our problems and work them through.

Love is freeing. Love is freely given, not doled out⑤ on demand. Authentic love is not given with strings attached. There is an unconditional quality about love.

Love is expansive. If I love you, I encourage you to reach out and develop other relationships. The honest evidence of our love is our commitment to encouraging another's full development.

Love means having a want for the person I love without having a need for that person in order to be complete. If I am nothing without you, then I'm not really free to love you.

Love means identifying⑥ with the person I love. If I love you, I can empathize with⑦ you and see the world through your eyes. I can identify with you because I'm able to see myself in you and you in me. This closeness does not imply a continual "togetherness", for distance and separation are sometimes essential in a loving relationship. Distance can intensify⑧ a loving bond, and it can help us rediscover ourselves, so that we are able to meet each other in a new way.

Love is selfish. I can only love you if I genuinely love, value,

---

① reciprocal[ri'siprəkəl] *adj.* 互惠的，相应的
② tolerate['tɔləreit] *v.* 忍受，容忍
③ impasse[æm'pɑːs; im'pæs] *n.* 僵局；绝境；死胡同
④ authentic[ɔː'θentik] *adj.* 可信的
⑤ dole out 少量地发放(食物、救济金等)
⑥ identify[ai'dentifai] *v.* 识别，鉴别
⑦ empathize with 同情
⑧ intensify[in'tensifai] *v.* 加强，强化

appreciate, and respect myself. If I am empty, the all I can give you is my emptiness. If I feel that I'm complete and worthwhile in myself, then I'm able to give you out of my fullness. One of the best ways for me to give you love is by fully enjoying myself with you.

Love involves seeing the potential① within the person we love. In my love for another, I view her or him as the person she or he can become, while still accepting who and what the person is now.

Mature love is union under the condition of preserving one's integrity②, one's individuality. In love this paradox③ occurs that two beings become one and yet remain two.

真爱的几点含义

爱意味着我了解我所爱的人。我清楚对方的许多方面——不仅仅是美好的一面，而且包括不足、矛盾和缺点。

爱意味着关心我所爱的人的幸福。如果我真关心你，就会关心你的成长，并希望你在一切可能的范围内成全自己。

爱意味着维护我所爱的人的尊严。如果我爱你，我就会把你看成一个独立的人，具有自己的价值观、思想和感情，而不会要求你为了我而改变你的个性并屈从于我对你的期待。

爱意味着对我所爱的人有责任心。如果我爱你，我会对你多数重要的个人需求作出反应。

爱意味着我和我所爱的人共同成长。如果我爱你，我就会因我的爱而在不断成长。你将会激励我更充分地发展我的潜能，而我对你的爱也将进一步完善你的整个人生。

爱意味着对我所爱的人做出某种承诺。这种承诺并非指我们之间要完

① potential[pəˈtenʃ(ə)l] *adj.* & *n.* 潜能，潜力

② integrity[inˈtegriti] *n.* 正直，诚实

③ paradox[ˈpærədɔks] *n.* 似是而非的论点，自相矛盾的话

全屈从于对方,也不隐含我们之间的关系一定要永久不变。它实指我们必须相互依存的愿望,不管是在平静和欢乐的日子,还是在痛苦、迷茫、挣扎和失望的时候,都不分离。

爱意味着信任我所爱的人。如果我爱你,我就会相信你会接受我的关怀和我的爱,也相信你不会故意伤害我。我相信我们的爱有一种互补的本质。

爱能容忍不完美。在相爱的过程中,肯定会出现厌烦的时候,有我想放弃的时候,有十分紧张的时候,亦有我感到无望的时候。真爱不意味着持久的幸福。然而,在厄境中我会坚持下去,因为我能记起我们在过去共同拥有的美好时光,也能预见,假如我们对自己的问题给予足够的重视并加以解决,我们会有光明的前景。

爱是自愿的。爱只能是无偿地献出,而不是在需要时的施舍。真爱的付出绝对没有任何附加条件,无条件才是爱的品质。

爱是扩展的。假如我爱你,我会鼓励你向外发展并建立其他人际关系。鼓励对方去充分发展自己才是两人相爱的真实证明。

爱意味着渴望得到我所爱的人,而不是因为缺了对方自己就会不完整。假如缺少你我就无法生存,那么我就不能尽情地去爱你。

爱意味着认同我所爱的人。如果我爱你,我会与你产生情感共鸣并能通过你的眼睛看世界。我之所以能认同你是因为你中有我,我中有你。此种亲密并不意味着两人一刻不能分离,因为离别和距离有时候在恋爱关系中是必要的。距离能加强爱的纽带,能帮助我们重新发现自己,因此我们能以某种新的方式认识对方。

爱是自我的。只有当我真正地爱自己、珍惜自己、欣赏并尊重自己,我才能爱你。假如我空虚,那么我能给予你的也只能是空虚。假如我觉得自己充实完整并活得有价值,那么我也能给予你充实完整。我给予你爱的最佳方式之一就是与你一起分享我的一切。

爱指的是能看清我们所爱的人的内在潜力。爱一个人时,我会一面接受对方的现状,一面把对方看成将来能成为的那种人。

成熟的爱是在保持个人完整独立性的前提下所形成的统一。合二为一,却又一分为二,这就是爱中似是而非的矛盾现象。

7. The Best Kind of Love

I have a friend who is falling in love. She honestly claims the sky is bluer. Mozart moves her to tears. She has lost 15 pounds and looks like a cover girl.

"I'm young again!" she shouts exuberantly①.

As my friend raves on about her new love, I've taken a good look at my old one. My husband of almost 20 years, Scott, has gained 15 pounds. Once a marathon② runner, he now runs only down hospital halls. His hairline is receding③ and his body shows the signs of long working hours and too many candy bars. Yet he can still give me a certain look across a restaurant table and I want to ask for the check and head home.

When my friend asked me "What will make this love last?" I ran through all the obvious reasons: commitment, shared interests, unselfishness, physical attraction, communication. Yet there's more. We still have fun. Spontaneous④ good times. Yesterday, after slipping the rubber band off the rolled up newspaper, Scott flipped it playfully at me: this led to an all-out war. Last Saturday at the grocery, we split the list and raced each other to see who could make it to the checkout first. Even washing dishes can be a blast. We enjoy simply being together.

And there are surprises. One time I came home to find a note on the front door that led me to another note, then another, until I reached the walk-in closet. I opened the door

① exuberantly[ig'zjuːbərəntli] *adv.* 丰富地，足够地，茂盛地

② marathon['mærəθən] *n.* [体]马拉松长跑

③ recede[ri'siːd] *v.* 后退

④ spontaneous[spɔn'teinjəs] *adj.* 自发的，自然产生的

to find Scott holding a "pot of gold" (my cooking kettle) and the "treasure" of a gift package. Sometimes I leave him notes on the mirror and little presents under his pillow.

There is understanding. I understand why he must play basketball with the guys. And he understands why, once a year, I must get away from the house, the kids—and even him—to meet my sisters for a few days of nonstop talking and laughing.

There is sharing. Not only do we share household worries and parental burdens—we also share ideas. Scott came home from a convention① last month and presented me with a thick historical novel. Though he prefers thrillers② and science fiction, he had read the novel on the plane. He touched my heart when he explained it was because he wanted to be able to exchange ideas about the book after I'd read it.

There is forgiveness. When I'm embarrassingly loud and crazy at parties, Scott forgives me. When he confessed losing some of our savings in the stock market, I gave him a hug and said, "It's okay. It's only money."

There is sensitivity③. Last week he walked through the door with that look that tells me it's been a tough day. After he spent some time with the kids, I asked him what happened. He told me about a 60-year-old woman who'd had a stroke. He wept as he recalled the woman's husband standing beside her bed, caressing her hand. How was he going to tell this husband of 40 years that his wife would probably never recover? I shed a few tears myself. Because of the medical crisis. Because there were still people who have been married 40 years. Because my husband is still moved and concerned after years of hospital rooms and dying patients.

There is faith. Last Tuesday a friend came over and confessed her fear that her husband is losing his courageous battle with cancer. On Wednesday I went to lunch with a friend who is struggling to reshape her

① convention[kən'venʃən] *n.* 大会,协定,习俗,惯例

② thriller['θrilə] *n.* 使人毛骨悚然的东西,使人毛骨悚然的小说

③ sensitivity[ˌsensi'tiviti] *n.* 敏感,灵敏(度),灵敏性

life after divorce. On Thursday a neighbor called to talk about the frightening effects of Alzheimer's disease on her father-in-law's personality. On Friday a childhood friend called long-distance to tell me her father had died. I hung up the phone and thought, this is too much heartache for one week. Through my tears, as I went out to run some errands①, I noticed the boisterous② orange blossoms of the gladiolus③ outside my window. I heard the delighted laughter of my son and his friend as they played. I caught sight of a wedding party emerging from a neighbor's house. The bride, dressed in satin and lace, tossed her bouquet④ to her cheering friends. That night, I told my husband about these events. We helped each other acknowledge the cycles of life and that the joys counter the sorrows. It was enough to keep us going.

Finally, there is knowing. I know Scott will throw his laundry just shy of the hamper every night; he'll be late to most appointments and eat the last chocolate in the box. He knows that I sleep with a pillow over my head; I'll lock us out of the house at a regular basis, and I will also eat the last chocolate.

I guess our love lasts because it is comfortable. No, the sky is not bluer: it's just a familiar hue. We don't feel particularly young: we've experienced too much that has contributed to our growth and wisdom⑤, taking its toll on our bodies, and created our memories.

I hope we've got what it takes to make our love last. As a bride, I had Scott's wedding band engraved⑥ with Robert Browning's line "Grow old along with me!" We're following those instructions.

If anything is real, the heart will make it plain.

---

① errand['erənd] *n.* 差事，差使，使命

② boisterous['bɔistərəs] *adj.* 狂暴的，喧闹的

③ gladiolus[ˌglædi'əuləs] *n.* [植]剑兰，唐菖蒲

④ bouquet['bu(:)kei, bu'kei] *n.* 花束

⑤ wisdom['wizdəm] *n.* 智慧，明智的行为

⑥ engrave[in'greiv] *v.* 雕刻

最真挚的爱

我有一个朋友坠入爱河。她发自内心地感叹，天空都变得更加蔚蓝！莫扎特的音乐会让她感动得流泪。她减重15磅，看起来像杂志上的封面女郎。

“我又年轻了！”她欢呼着。

当我朋友炫耀着她的新欢时，我开始好好地审视我的丈夫。结婚20年，斯科特增重15磅。以前的长跑爱好者，现在只是从家下楼跑到医院大厅。额头的发际线不断后移，从他的体型，你就可以看出他长期工作过量，吃糖太多。但是，在外吃饭时，坐在餐桌对面的他给我一个眼神，我就知道该结账回家了。

当我朋友问我“是什么让这份爱延续至今？”时，我很快罗列出显而易见的理由：责任感，共同的爱好，无私，身体的吸引，交流。还有其他很多原因。我们在一起感到发自内心的快乐。昨天，当斯科特取下卷报纸的皮筋，玩笑着把皮筋弹向我时，一场欢乐的“战争”全面爆发。上周六在食品店，我们把购物清单分两份，比赛谁能率先买好，并到收银台结账。甚至洗碗这样的小事也能让我们大乐一场。我们在一起享受着简单的快乐。

我们常常给对方惊喜。有一次回家，我发现门上有一张纸条，告诉我另一张纸条的位置，然后又是另一张，直到我走到壁橱。打开门，我发现斯科特捧着一个“金罐子”（我的蒸煮锅）和“财宝”礼包。有时候我也会把给他的纸条贴在镜子上，把送他的小礼物偷偷藏到他的枕头下。

我们相互理解。我理解为什么他一定要和他的朋友们一起打篮球，而他也理解为什么我每年都得离家几天，抛下孩子甚至他，和我的姐妹们小聚，叽叽咕咕聊天说笑。

我们共同分享。我们不仅一起分担琐碎的家务和为人父母的压力——我们还分享彼此的思想。上个月，斯科特开会回家，送给我一本厚厚的历史小说。虽然他一向喜欢的是恐怖和科幻小说，但是他却在飞机上阅读了这本小说。当他告诉我，他这样做是为了同我交流读书心得的时候,我深深地感动了。

我们宽容。当我在派对上不顾形象地高呼和狂欢时,斯科特不会责怪我。当他告诉我他在证券市场输掉了我们的部分积蓄时,我拥抱他,安慰道:"没事。钱财乃身外之物。"

我们都是性情中人。上周他下班回家时,我一看他的表情,就知道他心情沉重。在他陪孩子玩耍了一阵后,我问他发生了什么事情。他告诉我一个中风的60岁的老妇人的事。当说到老妇人的丈夫站在床边,抚摸她的手的情景,斯科特哭了。他怎么能告诉这个与妻子共度40年婚姻生活的老人,他的妻子再也不能康复了。我也忍不住掉下泪来。为折磨人的疾病;为这份40年的婚姻;为我的丈夫——在医院工作多年,见惯了垂危的生命,而他,依然有着易感和关怀病人的心。

我们都有坚定的信念。上周二,有位朋友来到我家,说她担心她的丈夫丧失与癌症病魔作战的勇气。周三,我跟一位刚离婚的朋友吃午餐,朋友正努力重新开始新的生活。周四,一位邻居打电话过来,告诉我老年痴呆症后给他的公公带来的可怕的影响。周五,一个儿时的伙伴打来长途,她的父亲离开了人世。挂了电话,我陷入了迷茫。一周发生了太多令人伤心的事情。泪眼模糊中,我走出去想做点什么,我看到了窗外怒放的橙色的剑兰。我听到了儿子和他的小伙伴们玩耍的欢声笑语。邻居家里正在举行婚宴,新娘子穿着蕾丝花边的绸缎婚纱,把手里的花束抛向欢呼的人群。那天晚上,我把这些事情告诉了丈夫。我们就这样相互搀扶着,体验生命的起起落落,让欢乐战胜忧伤,相濡以沫,白头偕老。

我们还相知相识。我知道每晚斯科特会把换洗的衣服扔向洗衣篓,却总扔不进去;约会时常常迟到,还会把盒子里最后一块巧克力给吃掉。他知道我睡觉时喜欢用枕头蒙住头;我经常忘记带钥匙,把我们自己锁在门外;还有我也会吃光最后一块巧克力。

我想,我们的爱情之所以长久,是因为我们在一起彼此都觉得很舒心。天空并没有变得格外的蓝:它还是我们熟悉的那种色彩。我们也不觉得自己变得特别年轻:我们一起经历了太多太多,这使我们更加成熟理智,虽然我们的身体日渐衰弱,但我们共同拥有了更多的回忆。

我希望我们已经获知了让爱永恒的真谛。我们结婚时,斯科特送给我刻有罗伯特·布朗宁"和我一起慢慢变老"诗句的婚戒。我们一直恪守着这句誓言。

如果真要说有什么变化的话,那就是心灵变得澄澈明净!

8. The Road to Happiness

It is a commonplace among moralists that you cannot get happiness by pursuing it. This is only true if you pursue it unwisely. Gamblers at Monte Carlo are pursuing money, and most of them lose it instead, but there are other ways of pursuing money, which often succeed. So it is with happiness. If you pursue it by means of drink, you are forgetting the hang-over. Epicurus pursued it by living only in congenial① society and eating only dry bread, supplemented by a little cheese on feast days. His method proved successful in his case, but he was a valetudinarian②, and most people would need something more vigorous. For most people, the pursuit of happiness, unless supplemented in various ways, is too abstract and theoretical to be adequate as a personal rule of life. But I think that whatever personal rule of life you may choose it should not, except in rare and heroic cases, be incompatible③ with happiness.

There are a great many people who have all the material conditions of happiness, i. e. health and a sufficient income, and who, nevertheless, are profoundly unhappy. In such cases it would seem as if the fault must lie with a wrong theory as to how to live. In one sense, we may say that any theory as to how to live is wrong. We imagine ourselves more different from the animals than we are. Animals live on impulse④, and are happy as long as external⑤ conditions are favorable. If you have a cat it will enjoy life if it has food and warmth and opportunities for an occasional night on the tiles. Your needs are more complex than those of your cat, but they still have their basis in instinct. In civilized societies, especially in English-speaking societies, this is too apt to be forgotten.

① congenial[kən'dʒiːnjəl] *adj.* 性情相似的，志趣相投的
② valetudinarian['væliˌtjuːdi'nεəriən] *n.* 体弱多病的人
③ incompatible[ˌinkəm'pætəbl] *adj.* 不相容的，不一致的
④ impulse['impʌls] *n.* 推动；冲动
⑤ external[eks'təːnl] *adj.* 外界的，客观的；外表的

People propose to themselves some one paramount① objective, and restrain all impulses that do not minister to it. A businessman may be so anxious to grow rich that to this end he sacrifices health and private affections. When at last he has become rich, no pleasure remains to him except harrying other people by exhortations② to imitate his noble example. Many rich ladies, although nature has not endowed them with any spontaneous③ pleasure in literature or art, decide to be thought cultured, and spend boring hours learning the right thing to say about fashionable new books that are written to give delight, not to afford opportunities for dusty snobbism④.

If you look around at the men and women whom you can call happy, you will see that they all have certain things in common. The most important of these things is an activity which at most gradually builds up something that you are glad to see coming into existence. Women who take an instinctive pleasure in their children can get this kind of satisfaction out of bringing up a family. Artists and authors and men of science get happiness in this way if their own work seems good to them. But there are many humbler forms of the same kind of pleasure. Many men who spend their working life in the city devote their weekends to voluntary and unremunerated⑤ toil in their gardens, and when the spring comes, they experience all the joys of having created beauty.

The whole subject of happiness has, in my opinion, been treated too

① paramount[ˈpærəmaunt] *adj.* 最高的,至上的,卓越的

② exhortation[ˌegzɔːˈteiʃən] *n.* 规劝,告诫

③ spontaneous[spɔnˈteinjəs] *adj.* 出自自然的,本能的

④ snobbism[ˈsnɔbizəm] *n.* 势利

⑤ unremunerate[ˈʌnriˈmjuːnəreit] *v.* 无酬报,无酬劳

solemnly①. It had been thought that man cannot be happy without a theory of life or a religion. Perhaps those who have been rendered unhappy by a bad theory may need a better theory to help them to recovery, just as you may need a tonic when you have been ill. But when things are normal a man should be healthy without a tonic and happy without a theory. It is the simple things that really matter. If a man delights in his wife and children, has success in work, and finds pleasure in the alternation of day and night, spring and autumn, he will be happy whatever his philosophy may be. If, on the other hand, he finds his wife fateful, his children's noise unendurable, and the office a nightmare; if in the daytime he longs for night, and at night sighs for the light of day, then what he needs is not a new philosophy but a new regimen②—a different diet, or more exercise, or what not.

Man is an animal, and his happiness depends on his physiology more than he likes to think. This is a humble conclusion, but I cannot make myself disbelieve it. Unhappy businessmen, I am convinced, would increase their happiness more by walking six miles every day than by any conceivable③ change of philosophy.

幸福之道

道德家们常说:幸福靠追求是得不到的。只有用不明智的方式去追求才是这样。蒙特卡洛城的赌徒们追求金钱,但多数人却把钱输掉了,而另外一些追求金钱的办法却常常成功。追求幸福也是一样。如果你通过畅饮来追求幸福,那你就忘记了酒醉后的不适。埃

① solemnly[ˈsɔləmli] *adv.* 严肃地,庄严地,隆重地
② regimen[ˈredʒimen] *n.* 摄生法,经系统安排的生活方式
③ conceivable[kənˈsiːvəbl] *adj.* 可想象的,可相信的

毕丘鲁斯追求幸福的办法是只和志趣相投的人一起生活，只吃不涂黄油的面包，节日才加一点奶酪。他的办法对他来说是成功的，但他是个体弱多病的人，而多数人需要的是精力充沛。就多数人来说，除非你有别的补充办法，这样追求快乐就过于抽象和脱离实际，不宜作为个人的生活准则。不过，我觉得无论你选择什么样的生活准则，除了那些罕见的和英雄人物的例子外，都应该是和幸福相容的。

很多人拥有获得幸福的全部物质条件，即健康的身体和丰足的收入，可是他们非常不快乐。就这种情况来说，似乎问题出在生活理论的错误上。从某种意义上讲，我们可以说任何关于生活的理论都是不正确的。我们和动物的区别并没有我们想象的那么大。动物是凭冲动生活的，只要客观条件有利，它们就会快乐。如果你有一只猫，它只要有东西吃，感到暖和，偶尔晚上得到机会去寻欢，它就会很快活。你的需要比你的猫要复杂一些，但还是以本能为基础的。在文明社会中，特别是在讲英语的社会中，这一点很容易被忘却。人们给自己定下一个最高的目标，对一切不利于实现这一目标的冲动都加以克制。生意人可能因为渴望发财以致不惜牺牲健康和爱情。等他终于发了财，他除了苦苦劝人效法他的好榜样而搅得别人心烦外，并没有得到快乐。很多有钱的贵妇人，尽管自然并未赋予她们任何欣赏文学或艺术的兴趣，却决意要使别人认为她们是有教养的，于是她们花费很多无聊的时间学习怎样谈论那些流行的新书。这些书写出来是要给人以乐趣的，而不是要给人以附庸风雅的机会的。

只要你观察一下周围那些你可称之为幸福的男男女女，就会看出他们都有某些共同之处。在这些共同之处中有一点是最重要的：那就是活动本身，它在大多数情况下本身就很有趣，而且可逐渐地使你的愿望得以实现。生性喜爱孩子的妇女，能够从抚养子女中得到这种满足。艺术家、作家和科学家如果对自己的工作感到满意，也能以同样的方式得到快乐。不过，还有很多是较低层次的快乐。许多在城里工作的人到了周末自愿在自家的庭院里做无偿的劳动，春天来时，他们就可尽情享受自己创造的美景带来的快乐。

在我看来，整个关于快乐的话题一向都被

太严肃地对待了。过去一直有这样的看法:如果没有一种生活的理论或者宗教信仰,人是不可能幸福的。也许那些由于理论不好才导致不快乐的人需要一种较好的理论帮助他们重新快活起来,就像你生过病需要吃补药一样。但是,正常情况下,一个人不吃补药也应当是健康的;没有理论也应当是幸福的。真正有关系的是一些简单的事情。如果一个男人喜爱他的妻子儿女,事业有成,而且无论白天黑夜,春去秋来,总是感到高兴,那么不管他的理论如何,都会是快乐的。反之,如果他讨厌自己的妻子,受不了孩子们的吵闹,而且害怕上班;如果他白天盼望夜晚,而到了晚上又巴望着天明,那么,他所需要的就不是一种新的理论,而是一种新的生活——改变饮食习惯,多锻炼身体等等。

人是动物,他的幸福更多的时候取决于其生理状况而非思想状况。这是一个很庸俗的结论,然而我无法使自己怀疑它。我确信,不幸福的商人与其找到新的理论来使自己幸福,还不如每天步行6英里更见效。

9. My Miraculous Family

I never considered myself unique①, but people are constantly telling me, "You are a miracle②." To me, I was just an ordinary "guy" with realistic goals and big dreams. I was a 19-year-old student at the University of Texas and well on my way toward fulfilling my "big dream" of one day becoming an orthopedic③ surgeon.

On the night of February 17, 1981, I was studying for an Organic Chemistry test at the library with Sharon, my girlfriend of three years. Sharon had asked me to drive her back to her dormitory as it was getting quite late. We got into my car, not realizing that just getting into a car would never quite be the same for me again. I quickly noticed that my gas gauge was registered on empty so I pulled into a nearby convenience store to buy $2.00 worth of gas. "I'll be back in two minutes," I yelled at Sharon as I closed the door. But instead, those two minutes changed my life forever.

Entering the convenience store was like entering the twilight zone. On the outside I was a healthy, athletic, pre-med student, but on the inside I was just another statistic of a violent crime. I thought I was entering an empty store, but suddenly I realized it was not empty at all. Three robbers were in the process of committing a robbery and my entrance into the store caught them by surprise. One of the criminals immediately shoved a .38 caliber④ handgun to my head,

① unique[juːˈniːk] *adj.* 唯一的，独特的

② miracle[ˈmirəkl] *n.* 奇迹，奇事

③ orthopedic[ˌɔːθəuˈpiːdik] (= orthopaedic) *adj.* [医]整形外科的

④ caliber[ˈkælibə(r)] *n.* 口径

ordered me to the cooler, pushed me down on the floor, and pumped a bullet into the back of my head—execution style. He obviously thought I was dead because he did not shoot me again. The trio of thieves finished robbing the store and left calmly.

Meanwhile, Sharon wondered why I had not returned. After seeing the three men leave the store she really began to worry as I was the last person she saw entering the store. She quickly went inside to look for me, but saw no one—only an almost empty cash register containing one check and several pennies. Quickly she ran down each aisle shouting, "Mike, Mike!"

Just then the attendant appeared from the back of the store shouting, "Lady, get down on the floor. I've just been robbed and shot at!"

Sharon quickly dropped to the floor screaming, "Have you seen my boyfriend? He has auburn hair." The man did not reply but went back to the cooler where he found me choking on my vomit①. The attendant quickly cleaned my mouth and then called for the police and an ambulance.

Sharon was in shock. She was beginning to understand that I was hurt, but she could not begin to comprehend② or imagine the severity③ of my injury.

When the police arrived they immediately called the homicide division as they did not think I would survive and the paramedic reported that she had never seen a person so severely wounded survive. At 1:30 a. m. my parents who lived in Houston, were

---

① vomit[ˈvɔmit] n. 呕吐,呕吐物,催吐剂

② comprehend[ˌkɔmpriˈhend] v. 领会,理解,包括,包含

③ severity[siˈveriti] n. 严肃,严格,严重

awakened by a telephone call from Brackenridge Hospital advising them to come to Austin as soon as possible for they feared I would not make it through the night.

But I did make it through the night and early in the morning the neurosurgeon① decided to operate. However, he quickly informed my family and Sharon that my chances of surviving the surgery were only 40—60%. If this were not bad enough, the neurosurgeon further shocked my family by telling them what life would be like for me if I beat the odds and survived. He said I probably would never walk, talk, or be able to understand even simple commands.

My family was hoping and praying to hear even the slightest bit of encouragement from that doctor. Instead, his pessimistic② words gave my family no reason to believe that I would ever again be a productive member of society. But once again I beat the odds and survived the three and a half hours of surgery.

Granted, I still could not talk, my entire right side was paralyzed③ and many people thought I could not understand, but at least I was stable. After one week in a private room the doctors felt I had improved enough to be transferred by jet ambulance④ to Del Oro Rehabilitation⑤ Hospital in Houston.

My hallucinations⑥, coupled with my physical problems, made my prognosis⑦ still very bleak. However, as time passed my mind began to clear and approximately six weeks later my right leg began to move ever so slightly. Within seven weeks my right arm slowly began to move and at eight weeks I uttered my first few words.

My speech was extremely difficult and slow in the beginning, but at

① neurosurgeon[ˌnjuərəu'səːdʒən] *n.* 神经外科医生

② pessimistic[ˌpesi'mistik] *adj.* 悲观的,厌世的

③ paralyze['pærəlaiz] *v.* 使瘫痪,使麻痹

④ ambulance['æmbjuləns] *n.* 救护车

⑤ rehabilitation['riː(h)əˌbili'teiʃən] *n.* 复原,康复

⑥ hallucination[həˌluːsi'neiʃən] *n.* 幻觉,幻想

⑦ prognosis[prɔg'nəusis] *n.* 预后

least it was a beginning. I was starting to look forward to each new day to see how far I would progress. But just as I thought my life was finally looking brighter I was tested by the hospital Europsychologist①. She explained to me that judging from my test results she believed that I should not focus on returning to college but that it would be better to set more "realistic goals".

Upon hearing her evaluation I became furious② for I thought, "Who is she to tell me what I can or cannot do. She does not even know me. I am a very determined and stubborn person!" I believe it was at that very moment that I decided I would somehow, someday return to college.

It took me a long time and a lot of hard work but I finally returned to the University of Texas in the fall of 1983—a year and a half after almost dying. The next few years in Austin were very difficult for me, but I truly believe that in order to see beauty in life you have to experience some unpleasantness. Maybe I have experienced too much unpleasantness, but I believe in living each day to the fullest, and doing the very best I can.

And each new day was very busy and very full, for besides attending classes at the University I underwent therapy③ three to five days each week at Brackenridge Hospital. If this were not enough I flew to Houston every other weekend to work with Tom Williams, a trainer and executive who had worked for many colleges and professional teams and also had helped many injured athletes, such as Earl Campbell and Eric Dickerson. Through Tom I learned: "Nothing is impossible and never, never give up or quit."

Early, during my therapy, my father kept repeating to me one of his favorite sayings. I have repeated it almost every day since being hurt: "Mile by mile it's a trial; yard by yard it's hard; but inch by inch it's a cinch."

I thought of those words, and I thought of Tom, my family and

① Europsychologist[ˌjuərəsaiˈkɔlədʒist] *n.* 欧洲来的心理学家

② furious[ˈfjuəriəs] *adj.* 狂怒的,狂暴的

③ therapy[ˈθerəpi] *n.* 治疗

Sharon who believed so strongly in me as I climbed the steps to receive my diploma from the Dean of Liberal Arts at the University of Texas on that bright sunny afternoon in June of 1986. Excitement and pride filled my heart as I heard the dean announce that I had graduated with "highest honors", been elected to Phi Beta Kappa, and been chosen as one of 12 Dean's Distinguished Graduates out of 1600 in the College of Liberal Arts.

The overwhelming emotions and feelings that I experienced at that very moment, when most of the audience gave me a standing ovation①, I felt it would never again be matched in my life—not even when I graduated with a master's degree in social work and not even when I became employed full time at the Texas Pain and Stress Center.

On May 24, 1987, I realized that nothing could ever match the joy I felt as Sharon and I were married. Sharon, my high school sweetheart of nine years, had always stood by me, through good and bad times. To me, Sharon is my miracle, my diamond in a world filled with problems, hurt, and pain. It was Sharon who dropped out of school when I was hurt so that she could constantly be at my side. She never wavered② or gave up on me.

It was her faith and love that pulled me through so many dark days. While other nineteen-year-old girls were going to parties and enjoying life, Sharon devoted her life to my recovery. That, to me, is the true definition of love.

After our beautiful wedding I continued working part time at the Pain Center and completed my work for a master's degree. We were extremely happy, but even happier when we learned Sharon was pregnant.

On July 11, 1990 at 12:15 a. m.

① ovation[əu'veiʃən] n. 热烈欢迎,欢呼

② wavered['weivəd] v. 犹豫

Sharon woke me with the news:"We need to go to the hospital my water just broke." I couldn't help but think how ironic it was that my life almost ended in a convenience store and now on the date "7 - 11" we were about to bring a new life into this world. This time it was my turn to help Sharon as she had helped me over those past years.

She was in labor for 15 hours. At 3:10 p. m. Sharon and I experienced the birth of our beautiful daughter, Shawn Elyse Segal!

Tears of joy and happiness came to my eyes as our healthy, alert, wonderful daughter entered this world. We anxiously counted her 10 fingers and her 10 toes and watched her wide eyes take in the world about her. It was truly a beautiful picture that was etched① in my mind forever as she lay in her mother's waiting arms, just minutes after her birth. At that moment I thanked God for blessing us with the greatest miracle of all—Shawn Elyse Segal.

我的神奇家庭

我从未觉得自己独特,但人们常对我说:“你是个奇迹。”对我而言,我只是一个普通人,有着现实的目标和远大的梦想。我曾是得克萨斯大学一名19 岁的大学生,在通向远大理想之路上信步前行,梦想有一天我会成为一名整形外科医生。

1981 年 2 月 17 日的晚上,我和交往三年的女友莎伦在图书馆里备考有机化学。因为太晚了,莎伦叫我驾车把她送回宿舍。我们钻进汽车,谁能想到在今后的生命中我再不能这样钻进汽车了。我很快发现油表空了,于是我把车泊在附近的一家便利店旁,想买两块钱的汽油。“我两分钟就回来,”我关上车门朝莎伦喊到。然而,就是这两分钟改变了我的一生。

进入这家便利店就如同踏上了阴阳间的奈何桥,门外的我还是个健康、有活力的医学预科生,而门内的我却成了暴力犯罪的又一个牺牲品。我还以为店里没有人,但我突然发现我错了——有三个匪徒正在打劫这家店,而我的进入让他们有些惊慌失措。其中一个匪徒迅速掏出一把口径为 38 毫米的手枪用力指着我的头,勒令我走到冷冻机旁,然后把我推倒在地,像执

① etched[ˈetʃid] *adj.* 被侵蚀的,被蚀刻的,风化的

行死刑般从后面朝我头部开了一枪。他没再朝我开第二枪，显然他以为我死了。打劫完后三个劫匪逃之夭夭。

与此同时，莎伦对我的不归忧心忡忡。看到这三个匪徒离开便利店后她真的很担心，因为我是她见到的最后一个进入店里的人。她赶快跑进店来找我，只见几乎被一扫而空的收银台上有一张支票和几枚硬币，四周无人。她在货架间飞快地跑着，喊着："迈克，迈克！"

这时一名服务员从店后面走出来叫到："小姐，趴到地板上。我刚才被打劫了，他们还向我开了枪。"

莎伦立即跪倒在地板上尖叫："你见到我的男朋友了吗？长褐色头发的。"那人没有回答，走到冷冻机旁，找到了我，此时呕吐快令我窒息了。他赶忙帮我擦干了嘴，叫了警察和救护车。

莎伦被吓坏了，渐渐地她才明白我受伤了，但是她根本想象不到伤势的严重程度。

警察来了，他们立即给凶杀组打电话，他们不能想象我还能活过来，而救护人员说她从来没有见过伤势如此严重的人可以死里逃生。凌晨一点半，我住在休斯敦的父母被来自布莱肯瑞吉医院的电话铃惊醒，医院通知他们尽快赶到奥斯汀，因为他们认为我熬不过当晚了。

但那晚我挺了过来，第二天清晨神经外科医生决定给我动手术。然而，他立即告知我的家人和莎伦我的手术存活机会只有百分之四十到六十。然后，他还雪上加霜地告诉我的家人，向他们描述如果我万幸活下来将面临怎样的生活——我可能再也不会走路了，不会说话了，甚至不能理解一些简单的命令。

我的家人本来祈望能从医生的口中听到一点点鼓励的话，而他悲观的言语让他们没理由相信我还会成为一个对社会有用的人。在经历了三个半小时的手术之后，我再次侥幸地活了下来。

医生的话得到了应验，我不能说话，整个右边的身体瘫痪了，许多人认为我变傻了，但至少我身体状况是稳定的。在私人看护病房里呆了一个星期后，医生觉得我已经好转了许多，并可以坐救护飞机转到休斯敦的德欧洛康复医院。

意识上的幻觉和生理上的病疾使我的病情预后非常渺茫。然而，随着时间的过往，我的头脑开始清醒了，大约6个星期以后我的右腿可以轻微地活动了，7周以后我的右臂开始缓慢地活动了，8周以后我说出了几个词。

开始时,我说话非常困难,语速很慢。但是总算是开头了。我开始指望着每过一天我能取得多大进步。但正当我以为生活总算初露光明的时候,医院里有个欧洲来的心理学家对我做了测试。她向我解释,从检测的结果来看她认为我不能再重返学校,劝我对此不要抱有任何希望,希望我最好树立些更"现实的目标"。

她的这番评论让我怒不可遏,"她是谁,凭什么告诉我能做什么或不能做什么。她根本不了解我。我是个很坚强很固执的人!"我相信就在那时我决定无论如何,总有一天我会返回学校的。

在经历了一年半垂死挣扎的生活后,在漫长的等待和艰辛的付出后,终于在 1983 年的秋天,我返回了得克萨斯大学。在奥斯汀接下来的几年里我生活得非常艰难,但我确信为了看到生活中的真善美你必须要经历一些苦难。也许我经历的苦难太多了,但我有一个信念——充实地过每一天,尽力做到最好。

每一天都过得很繁忙、很充实,除了在大学上课,每周我还要在布莱肯瑞吉医院接受三到五天的治疗。如果这还不够忙的话,我还要隔周周末飞到休斯敦和汤姆 · 威廉斯一起工作。汤姆是一个教练兼主管,他曾效力于许多大学校队和职业球队,并帮助过许多受伤的运动员,如:厄尔 · 坎贝尔和埃里克 · 迪克森。从汤姆的身上我学到"没有什么是不可能的,永不让步,永不放弃"。

早在我接受治疗的时候,父亲总是重复他最爱的那句话。自从受伤之后我几乎每天都对自己重复那句话,那就是"一里可尝行,一码尚难行,一寸才是金"。

1986 年 6 月那个阳光明媚的午后,当我爬上得克萨斯大学的台阶从文学院院长手中接过文凭时,我思索着这些话,想到汤姆、家人,还有莎伦,他们都那么坚定地给予了我信任。当我听到院长宣布我以最高荣誉毕业时,我的心中充满了骄傲和兴奋。接着,他还宣布我被选入美国大学优等生荣誉学会,并在 1600 名毕业生中当选为 12 名文学院的杰出毕业生之一。

当场有许多观众站起来为我欢呼,那一刻令我心潮澎湃、百感交集。我甚至觉得生命中不可能再经历那样的感慨和激情,这种想法一直延续到我获得社会学的硕士学位,成为得克萨斯止痛减压中心的一名全职工作人员。

1987 年 5 月 24 日,我觉得再没有什么能与此时的快乐相提并论,我和莎伦结婚了。莎伦是我高中时代的女友,风风雨雨 9 年来,她一直陪在我身旁。对我来说,莎伦是我的奇迹,是我在这个充满困惑和伤痛的世界上拥有的一颗钻石。为了能日夜守候在我的身旁，莎伦在我受伤的时候放弃了学业。她的爱从未动摇过，她从未抛弃过我。

是她的忠诚和爱伴着我度过了无数个黑暗的日子。当别的19岁的女孩子参加舞会、享受生活的时候，莎伦把青春献给了我，等待我的康复。对我来说，这就是爱的真谛。

在那个美满的婚礼之后，我继续在止痛中心做着兼职的工作，并完成我的硕士学位学习。我们非常幸福，而莎伦怀孕的消息更让我们恩爱有加。

1990年7月11日12点15分，莎伦把我从梦中唤醒："我们得去医院了……我羊水破了。"我忍不住在想命运真让人啼笑皆非，它几乎让我在那家便利店里丢了性命，而在一个命名为"7·11"的日子里它却让我迎来新生命的出世。多年来莎伦帮我渡过了一次又一次难关，这次该我来帮助她了。

莎伦经历了15个小时的分娩。在下午3点10分的时候，莎伦和我一起迎来了我们美丽的女儿——萧恩·艾丽斯·斯高！

当我看到健康、聪明、可爱的女儿来到这个世上时，喜悦和幸福的泪水夺眶而出。我们迫不及待地数着她的十个手指和十只脚趾，看着她大大的眼睛注视着她周围的世界。初生的婴儿躺在妈妈柔软的怀里如一幅优美的图画将永驻我的心中。那一刻，我感谢上帝赐予我们如此伟大的奇迹——我的萧恩·艾丽斯·斯高。

10. If the Dream Is Big Enough

I used to watch her from my kitchen window, she seemed so small as she muscled her way through① the crowd of boys on the playground. The school was across the street from our home and I would often watch the kids as they played during recess. A sea of children, and yet to me, she stood out from them all.

I remember the first day I saw her playing basketball. I watched in wonder as she ran circles around the other kids. She managed to shoot jump shots just over their heads and into the net. The boys always tried to stop her but no one could.

I began to notice her at other times, basketball in hand, playing alone. She would practice dribbling② and shooting over and over again, sometimes until dark. One day I asked her why she practiced so much. She looked directly in my eyes and without a moment of hesitation she said, "I want to go to college. The only way I can go is if I get a scholarship. I like basketball. I decided that if I were good enough, I would get a scholarship. I am going to play college basketball. I want to be the best. My Daddy told me if the dream is big enough, the facts don't count. "Then she smiled and ran towards the court to recap③ the routine I had seen over and over again.

Well, I had to give it to her—she was determined. I watched her through those junior high years and into high school. Every week, she led her varsity④ team to victory.

One day in her senior year, I saw her sitting in the grass, head cradled in her arms. I walked across the street and sat down in the cool grass beside her. Quietly I asked what was wrong. "Oh, nothing," came a

---

① muscled her way through 她跻身于
② dribble['dribl]v. 带球,运球
③ recap['riːkæp, riː'kæp]v. 又开始
④ varsity['vɑːsiti]n. 大学运动代表队,大学

soft reply. "I am just too short." The coach told her that at 5'5 she would probably never get to play for a top ranked team—much less offered a scholarship—so she should stop dreaming about college.

She was heartbroken and I felt my own throat tighten as I sensed her disappointment. I asked her if she had talked to her dad about it yet.

She lifted her head from her hands and told me that her father said those coaches were wrong. They just did not understand the power of a dream. He told her that if she really wanted to play for a good college, if she truly wanted a scholarship, that nothing could stop her except one thing—her own attitude. He told her again, "If the dream is big enough, the facts don't count."

The next year, as she and her team went to the Northern California Championship game, she was seen by a college recruiter①. She was indeed offered a scholarship, a full ride, to a Division I, NCAA② women's basketball team. She was going to get the college education that she had dreamed of and worked toward for all those years.

It's true: If the dream is big enough, the facts don't count.

只要梦想足够远大

我过去常常从厨房的窗户看到她跻身于操场上的一群男孩子中间，她显得那么矮小。学校在我家的街对面，我可以经常看到孩子们在下课时间打球。尽管有一大群的孩子，但我觉得她跟其他的孩子截然不同。

我记得第一天看到她打篮球的情景。看着她在其他孩子旁边兜来转去，我感到十分惊奇。她总是尽力地跳起投篮，球恰好越过那些孩子的头顶飞入篮筐。那些男孩总是拼命地阻止她，但没有人能做到。

我开始注意到她有时候一个人打球。她一遍遍地练习带球和投篮，有时直到天黑。一天，我问她为什么这么刻苦地练习。她直视着我的眼睛，毫不犹豫地说："我想上大学。只有获得奖学金我才能上大学。我喜欢打篮球，我想只要我打得好，我就能获得奖学金。我要到大学去打篮球。我想成

① recruiter[riˈkruːtə] n. 招聘人员

② NCAA: abbr. National Collegiate Athletic Association（美国）全国大学生体育协会

为最棒的球员。我爸爸告诉我,只要梦想足够远大,过程不在话下。"说完她笑了笑,跑向篮球场,又开始我之前见过的一遍又一遍的常规练习。

我真是服了她了——她是下定了决心。我看着她这些年从初中升到高中。每个星期,她带领的学校篮球代表队都能够获胜。

她读高中的一天,我看见她坐在草地上,头埋在臂弯里。我穿过街道,坐到她旁边清凉的草地上。我轻轻地问出什么事了。"哦,没什么,"她轻声回答,"只是我太矮了。"原来篮球教练告诉她,以五英尺五英寸的身材,她几乎是没有机会到一流的球队去打球的——更不用说会获得奖学金了——所以她应该放弃想上大学的梦想。

她很伤心,我感觉到了她的失望,我也觉得自己的喉咙发紧。我问她是否与她的爸爸谈过这件事。

她从臂弯里抬起头,告诉我,她爸爸说那些教练错了。他们根本不懂得梦想的力量。他告诉她,如果她真的想到一所好的大学去打篮球,如果她真的想获得奖学金,任何东西也不能阻止她,除非她自己不愿意。他又一次跟她说:"只要梦想足够远大,过程不在话下。"

第二年,当她和她的球队去参加北加利福尼亚州冠军赛时,她被一位大学的招生人员看中了。她真的获得了奖学金,一个全面资助的奖学金,并且进入美国全国大学体育协会中的女子甲组篮球队。她将接受她曾梦想并为之奋斗多年的大学教育。

是的,只要梦想足够远大,过程不在话下。

11. You Don't Love me

"You don't love me!"

How many times have your kids laid that one on you?

And how many times have you, as a parent, resisted the urge to tell them how much?

Someday, when my children are old enough to understand the logic that motivates① a mother, I'll tell them.

I loved you enough to bug you about where you were going, with whom, and what time you would get home.

I loved you enough to insist you buy a bike with your own money that we could afford and you couldn't.

I loved you enough to be silent and let you discover your hand-picked friend was a creep.

I loved you enough to make you return a Milky Way with a bite out of it to a drugstore and confess, "I stole this."

I loved you enough to stand over you for two hours while you cleaned your bedroom, a job that would have taken me fifteen minutes.

I loved you enough to say, "Yes, you can go to Disney World on Mother's Day."

I loved you enough to let you see anger, disappointment, disgust② and tears in my eyes.

I loved you enough not to make excuses for your lack of respect or your bad manners.

I loved you enough to admit that I was wrong and ask your

① motivate['məutiveit]v. 激发

② disgust[dis'gʌst]n. 厌恶,嫌恶

forgiveness.

I loved you enough to ignore "what every other mother" did or said.

I loved you enough to let you stumble, fall, hurt and fail.

I loved you enough to let you assume the responsibility for your own actions, at six, ten, or sixteen.

I loved you enough to figure you would lie about the party being chaperoned①, but forgave you for it... after discovering I was right.

I loved you enough to shove you off my lap, let go of your hand, be mute to your pleas...so that you had to stand alone.

I loved you enough to accept you for what you are, not what I wanted you to be.

But most of all, I loved you enough to say no when you hated me for it. That was the hardest part of all.

你不爱我

"你不爱我!"

你的孩子有多少次这样对你讲这句话?

而你,作为一个父母,有多少次不愿意说出你有多爱他?

等到有一天,我的孩子长大,能够理解那种激发一位母亲的逻辑的时候,我就会告诉他们。

我是如此地爱着你,所以想知道你要去哪里,和谁在一起,以及回家的时间。

我是如此地爱着你,所以坚持让你用自己的钱去买一辆自行车,尽管我们买得起而你却望尘莫及。

我是如此地爱着你,所以让你自己去发现你交的朋友是位马屁精,而我却沉默无声。

我是如此地爱着你,所以让你把咬了一口的奶油面包还给杂货店,然后承认:"我偷的。"

我是如此地爱着你,所以在你

① chaperone['ʃæpərəun]v. 伴护

打扫你的卧室的时候，我站在一旁看了整整两个小时，尽管我用一刻钟就能把它收拾完毕。

我是如此地爱着你，所以对你说，“好的，你可以在母亲节那天去迪斯尼乐园。”

我是如此地爱着你，所以让你从我的眼睛中看到愤怒、失望、厌恶和泪水。

我是如此地爱着你，所以在你不尊重别人或者表现粗鲁的时候，没有为你寻找任何借口。

我是如此地爱着你，所以我会承认错误来得到你的宽恕。

我是如此地爱着你，所以对“其他母亲”说的或做的并不在意。

我是如此地爱着你，所以让你自己绊倒，摔跤，受伤或者失败。

我是如此地爱着你，所以让你为自己的行为负责任，无论你是 6 岁，10 岁还是 16 岁。

我是如此地爱着你，所以猜出你在舞会上有女伴是个谎言，在发现我的猜测是事实后却原谅了你。

我是如此地爱着你，所以让你从我的怀抱离开，放开你的手，对你的请求无动于衷……就是为了能够让你自立。

我是如此地爱着你，所以接受原原本本的你，而不是我期望中的你。

然而，更要紧的是，我是如此地爱着你，尽管你会恨我这么做，我还是对你说“不”。这就是我所有的对待你的行为中最难做到的部分。

12. Your Mind Is a Garden

Some time ago, Sofan and I were visiting some friends in the country. We were staying in a beautiful little guest cabin, surrounded by fruit trees, flowers and even a few goats. Painted above the doorway in brightly colored, flowing letters were the words:

Your mind is a garden.
Your thoughts are the seeds.
You can grow flowers or
You can grow weeds…

Little did we know it at the time, but this little poem was to have a profound① effect both on our thought patterns as well as our artworks.

It started almost as a kind of game. We decided to make a real effort to watch our thoughts and see exactly what it was that we were planting in our own "Mind Gardens". It was difficult at first, but gradually, we began to pay more and more attention to what thoughts were repeatedly flashing across our minds.

How disturbing it was to discover that many of these "seeds" were extremely negative thoughts destined to grow patches of thorny② thistles and stinging nettles in our daily lives!

We gradually came to see how so many of the problems and difficulties we were encountering in our lives had their beginnings in the seeds of doubt, fear and anxiety that we were continually planting in our minds.

It does take effort, but like anything else it gets easier with practice, and the amazing thing is, as we become more and more aware of③ these negative thoughts we are able to say:

"No! I will NOT plant this weed in the Garden of my Mind."

① profound[prə'faund] *adj.* 深刻的,意义深远的
② thorny['θɔːni] *adj.* 多刺的,痛苦的
③ aware of 意识到

I will consciously choose to plant something better. The results are truly spectacular.

When you start to consciously cultivate① your own mind garden, you will truly be amazed at the changes which begin to happen in your life. Obstacles disappear, barriers fall away, and things that you once thought were either impossible or very far away will suddenly come into view.

Any garden is an ongoing process. It's not enough to just plant a single seed of happiness and then forget about it. Your frail② little seedling③ would soon be choked by weeds. It is necessary to continuously pull out and throw away those weeds of fear, doubt and anxiety④ as soon as they appear.

Love, happiness and tranquility⑤ are all contagious⑥. People who are continuously planting these seeds in their own minds are also planting them in other people.

Remember,

Your mind is a garden.

Your thoughts are the seeds.

You can grow flowers or

You can grow weeds...

So ask yourself, what are you going to grow in the glorious⑦ garden of your mind? May your life be filled with love, happiness and inspiration⑧.

---

① cultivate[ˈkʌltiveit] *v.* 培养

② frail[freil] *adj.* 虚弱的，脆弱的

③ seedling[ˈsiːdliŋ] *n.* 秧苗，树苗

④ anxiety[æŋɡˈzaiəti] *n.* 忧虑，焦急

⑤ tranquility[træŋˈkwiliti] *n.* 宁静

⑥ contagious[kənˈteidʒəs] *adj.* 传染性的，会感染的

⑦ glorious[ˈɡlɔːriəs] *adj.* 光荣的，显赫的

⑧ inspiration[ˌinspəˈreiʃən] *n.* 灵感

心如花园

不久前，我和索芳到乡间访友，暂居在一个给客人住的小木屋里。木屋很漂亮，四周有果树和花朵环绕，甚至还有几只山羊。屋门上几行漆字，颜色鲜亮，字体流畅。写的是：

心如花园，
思想为种。
可生花束，
或生草丛……

当时我们不甚懂得这首小诗，但后来它却给我们的思维模式与艺术作品带来了深远的影响。

刚开始的时候几乎就像一场游戏。我们决定下一番真功夫去观察自己的思想，把我们在自己"心之花园"里种下的东西看个真切。起初并不容易，但渐渐地，我们开始愈发关注在自己心中反复闪过的是何种思想。

当发现大多数的"思之种子"都是很负面的思想，注定要在我们的日常生活中长成一丛丛带刺的野蓟、荨麻的时候，这是多么让人烦恼啊！

我们渐渐发现，我们在生活中遇到的诸多问题与困难，其源头正是我们不断在心中种下的疑惑、恐惧与焦虑的种子。

这的确是件费劲的事，但跟其他所有事一样，它也是熟能生巧，令人惊异的是，当我们越来越意识到这些负面的思想时，我们就能说：

"不！我不会把这棵杂草种在我的心园。"

我会有意识地去选择种一些更好的东西，收获颇丰。

当你开始有意识地去耕作自己的心之花园时，生命中因此发生的改变会令你大为惊异。障碍消失了，隔阂不见了，你一度认为不可能或离你很遥远的事情突然展现在你眼前。

每一个花园都处在不断变化之中。仅种下一棵幸福的种子，接着又抛之脑后是不行的。你那孱弱的秧苗很快就会被野稗吞噬。那些恐惧、疑惑与焦虑的野稗一长出来，就要持之以恒地把它们拔除扔掉。

爱、幸福与宁静都是有感染力的。那些在自己心园里不断播种这些种子的人们，他们也会把爱、幸福与宁静种到别人的心里去。

请记住：

心如花园，

思想为种。

可生花束，

或生草丛……

故而问问自己，你会在自己绚丽的心园里种些什么呢？愿你的生活充满爱、幸福与灵感。

13. Learn to Live in the Present Moment

To a large degree, the measure of our peace of mind is determined by how much we are able to live in the present moment. Irrespective① of what happened yesterday or last year, and what may or may not happen tomorrow, the present moment is where you are—always!

Without question, many of us have mastered the neurotic art of our lives worrying about a variety of things—all at once. We allow past problems and future concerns to dominate② our present moments, so much that we end up anxious, frustrated, depressed, and hopeless. On the flip side, we also postpone③ our gratification④, our stated priorities⑤, and our happiness, often convincing ourselves future will be better than today. Unfortunately, the same mental dynamics that tell us to look toward to the future will only repeat themselves so that "someday" never actually arrives. John Lennon once said, "Life is what's happening while we're busy making other plans." When we're busy making "other plans", our children are busy growing up, the people we love are moving away and dying, our bodies are getting out of shape, and our dreams are slipping away⑥. In short, we miss out on life.

Many people live as if life were a dress rehearsal⑦ for some later date. It isn't. In fact, no one has a guarantee⑧ that he or she will be here tomorrow. Now is the only time we have, and the only time that we have any control over. When our attention is in the present moment, we push fear from our minds. Fear is the concern over events that might happen in

① irrespective[ˌiris'pektiv] *adj.* 不顾的,不考虑的
② dominate['dɔmineit] *v.* 支配,占优势
③ postpone[pəust'pəun] *v.* 推迟,使延期,延迟
④ gratification[ˌgrætifi'keiʃən] *n.* 满意
⑤ priority[prai'ɔriti] *n.* 优先,优先权
⑥ slip away 消失
⑦ rehearsal[ri'həːsəl] *n.* 排演,演习,预演,试演
⑧ guarantee[ˌgærən'tiː] *n.* 保证

the future—we won't have enough money, our children will get into trouble, we will get old and die, whatever.

学会生活在此时

在很大程度上,我们内心的平和取决于我们在多大程度上生活在此时。不管昨天或去年发生了什么,也不管明天将会发生什么或不会发生什么,此时才是你所在之处——永远是这样!

毫无疑问,在我们的生活中,许多人总是这样的神经兮兮,担心着各种各样的事情,而且会突然之间一齐涌上心头。我们让过去与未来的问题支配我们现有的时间,以至于整日焦躁不安、委靡不振、精神沮丧甚至感到绝望。另一方面,我们又永远不让自己满足,不去享有优先权和幸福感,而且还经常说服自己将来会比今天好。不幸的是,同样的告诉我们去展望未来的精神动力只是不断重复自己,以至于"某一天"永远不能到来。约翰·列侬曾说:"生活就是我们忙于制订其他计划时所发生的事。"当我们忙于制订"其他计划"时,我们的孩子忙于成长,我们所爱之人远离并撒手尘寰,我们体型走样了,我们的梦想消失了。总之,我们错过了人生的大好光阴。

许多人活着,他们的生活就像未来日子的一次彩排。然而,并非如此。事实上,没有人能确保他或她明天还在。现在是我们拥有的唯一时间,是唯一能够把握的时间。当我们的注意力集中于现在时,我们便能消除恐惧。恐惧是我们对未来事情的担心,比如我们没有足够的钱,我们的孩子会惹上麻烦,我们会变老,会离开人世,如此等等。

14. Life Is to Be Whole

Once a circle missed a wedge①. The circle wanted to be whole, so it went around looking for its missing piece. But because it was incomplete and therefore could roll only very slowly, it admired the flowers along the way. It chatted with worms. It enjoyed the sunshine. It found lots of different pieces, but none of them fit. So it left them all by the side of the road and kept on searching. Then one day the circle found a piece that fit perfectly. It was so happy. Now it could be whole, with nothing missing. It incorporated② the missing piece into itself and began to roll. Now that it was a perfect circle, it could roll very fast, too fast to notice the flowers or talk to the worms. When it realized how different the world seemed when it rolled so quickly, it stopped, left its found piece by the side of the road and rolled slowly away.

The lesson of the story, I suggested, was that in some strange sense we are more whole when we are missing something. The man who has everything is in some ways a poor man. He will never know what it feels like to yearn, to hope, to nourish his soul with the dream of something better. He will never know the experience of having someone who loves him and gives him something he has always wanted or never had.

There is a wholeness about the person who has come to terms with his limitations, who has been brave enough to let go of his unrealistic③ dreams and not feel like a failure for doing so. There is a wholeness about the man or woman who has learned that he or she is strong enough to go through a tragedy and survive, who can lose someone and still feel like a complete person.

① wedge[wedʒ] *n.* 楔,楔形物

② incorporate[inˈkɔːpəreit] *vt.* 结合,合并

③ unrealistic[ˈʌnriəˈlistik] *adj.* 不切实际的,不实在的

Life is not a trap set for us by God so that he can condemn us for failing. Life is not a spelling bee, where no matter how many words you have gotten right; you are disqualified① if you make one mistake. Life is more like a baseball season, where even the best team loses one-third of its games and even the worst team has its days of brilliance②. Our goal is to win more games than we lose.

When we accept that imperfection is part of being human, and when we can continue rolling through life and appreciate it, we will have achieved a wholeness that others can only aspire to. That, I believe, is what God asks of us—not "Be perfect", not "Don't even make a mistake", but "Be whole".

If we are brave enough to love, strong enough to forgive, generous enough to rejoice in another's happiness, and wise enough to know there is enough love to go around for us all, then we can achieve a fulfillment③ that no other living creature will ever know.

人生在于完整

从前一只圆圈缺了一个楔子，它想保持完整，便四处寻找失去的那块楔子。由于它不完整，滚动很慢，所以一路上它很羡慕花儿。它与蠕虫谈天侃地，还享受到了阳光。它找到了许许多多不同配件，但没有一件适合。所以它将它们统统弃之路旁，继续寻找。终于有一天，它找到了一个完美的配件。圆圈是那样的高兴，现在它可以说是完美无缺了。它装好配件，然后滚动起来。既然它成了完美的圆圈，所以滚动得特别快，快得无暇观赏花儿，无暇与蠕虫交谈。圆圈急速奔驰，发现眼中的世界如此不同，于是，它不禁停了下来，将找到的那个配件留在路旁，又开始慢慢地滚动。

我觉得这个故事告诉了我们，从某种奇特的意义上讲，当我们失去一些东西时反而感到更加完整。一个拥有一切的人在某些方面是个穷人，他永远也体会不到什么是渴望，什么是期待，也永远感悟不到美好的梦想。他也

① disqualify[dis'kwɔlifai] *v.* 使丧失资格

② brilliance['briljəns] *n.* 光辉，显赫，鲜明

③ fulfillment[ful'filmənt] *n.* 履行，实行

永远不会有这样一种体验:一个爱他的人送给他某种他梦寐以求的或者从未拥有过的东西意味什么。

一个人的完整性在于他知道如何面对他的缺陷,如何勇敢地摈弃那些不现实的幻想而又不以此为缺憾。人的完整性还在于一个男人或女人懂得这样一个道理:他/她发现自己能勇敢面对人生悲剧而继续生存,能够在失去亲人后依然表现出一个完整的人的风范。

人生不是上帝为谴责我们的堕落而设的陷阱。人生也不是一场拼字游戏比赛,不管你拼出多少个单词,一旦出现一个错误,你就前功尽弃。人生更像是一个棒球赛季,即使再好的球队也会输掉1/3,而再差的球队也有春风得意的日子。我们的目标就是多赢球,少输球。

当我们接受了不完整性是人性的一部分时,当我们不断地进行人生滚动并能意识其价值时,我们就会完成完整人生的过程,而对于别人来讲,这只是一个梦想。我相信这就是上帝对我们的要求:不求"完美",也不求"永不犯错",而是求得人生的"完整"。

如果我们勇敢得能够去爱,坚强得能够去宽容,大度得能够去分享他人的幸福,明智得能够理解身边充满爱,那么我们就能取得别的生物所不能取得的成就。

15. The Marks of Life

My teammates on the United States Disabled Ski Team used to tease me about the size of my chest, joking that my greatest handicap wasn't my missing leg but my missing cleavage①. Little did they know how true that would become. This past year, I found out that for the second time in my life I had cancer, this time in both breasts. I had bilateral② mastectomies③.

When I heard I'd need the surgery, I didn't think it would be a big deal. I even told my friends playfully, "I'll keep you abreast of the situation." After all, I had lost my leg to my first go-round with cancer at age 12, then gone on to become a world-champion ski racer. All of us on the Disabled Ski Team were missing one set of body parts or another. I saw that a man in a wheelchair can be utterly sexy. That a woman who has no hands can appear not to be missing anything. That wholeness has nothing to do with missing parts and everything to do with spirit. Yet although I knew this, I was surprised to discover how difficult it was to adjust④ to my new scars.

When they brought me back to consciousness⑤ after the surgery, I started to sob and hyperventilate⑥. Suddenly I found that I didn't want to face the loss of more of my body. I didn't want chemotherapy⑦

---

① cleavage[ˈkliːvidʒ] *n.* 劈开,分裂
② bilateral[baiˈlætərəl] *adj.* 有两面的,双边的
③ mastectomy[mæsˈtektəmi] *n.* 乳房切除术
④ adjust[əˈdʒʌst] *v.* 调整,调节
⑤ consciousness[ˈkɔnʃəsnis] *n.* 意识,知觉
⑥ hyperventilate[ˌhaipə(ː)ventiˈleit] *v.* [医]换气过度,强力呼吸
⑦ chemotherapy[ˌkeməuˈθerəpi] *n.* 化学疗法

again. I didn't want to be brave and tough and put on a perpetual① smiling face. I didn't ever want to wake up again. My breathing grew so shaky that the anesthesiologist② gave me oxygen and then, thankfully, put me back to sleep.

When I was doing hill sprints to prepare for my ski racing—my heart and lungs and leg muscles all on fire—I'd often be hit by the sensation③ that there were no resources left inside me with which to keep going. Then I'd think about the races ahead—my dream of pushing my potential④ as far as it could go, the satisfaction of breaking through my own barriers—and that would get me through the sprints. The same tenacity⑤ that served me so well in ski racing helped me survive my second bout with cancer.

After the mastectomies, I knew that one way to get myself going would be to start exercising again, so I headed for the local pool. In the communal⑥ shower, I found myself noticing other women's breasts for the first time in my life. Size-D breasts and size-A breasts, sagging⑦ breasts and perky⑧ breasts. Suddenly and for the first time, after all these years of missing a leg, I felt acutely self-conscious. I couldn't bring myself to undress.

I decided it was time to confront myself. That night at home, I took off all my clothes and had a long look at the woman in the mirror. She was androgynous⑨. Take my face—without makeup, it was a cute young boy's face. My shoulder muscles, arms and hands were powerful and

① perpetual[pə'petjuəl] *adj.* 永久的
② anesthesiologist['ænisˌθizi'ɔlədʒist] *n.* 麻醉师
③ sensation[sen'seiʃən] *n.* 感觉,感情
④ potential[pə'tenʃ(ə)l] *n.* 潜能
⑤ tenacity[ti'næsiti] *n.* 坚韧
⑥ communal['kɔmjunl] *adj.* 公共的,公社的
⑦ sagging['sægiŋ] *adj.* 下垂的
⑧ perky['pəːki] *adj.* 自信的,得意洋洋的
⑨ androgynous[æn'drɔdʒinəs] *adj.* 雌雄同体的

muscular from the crutches. I had no breasts; instead, there were two prominent① scars on my chest. I had a sexy flat stomach, a bubble butt and a well-developed thigh from years of ski racing. My right leg ended in another long scar just above the knee.

I discovered that I liked my androgynous body. It fits my personality—my aggressive② male side that loves getting dressed in a helmet, arm guards and shin protectors to do battle with the slalom③ gates, and my gentle female side that longs to have children one day and wants to dress up in a beautiful silk dress, go out to dinner with a lover and then lie back and be slowly undressed by him.

I found that the scars on my chest and my leg were a big deal. They were my marks of life. All of us are scarred by life; it's just that some of those scars show more clearly than others. Our scars do matter. They tell us that we have lived, that we haven't hidden from life. When we see our scars plainly, we can find in them, as I did that day, our own unique④ beauty.

The next time I went to the pool I showered naked.

生命的印记

我在美国残疾人滑雪队的队友们经常拿我的乳房尺寸开玩笑，他们说我最大的不足不是因为没了一条腿，而是因为少了一条沟（乳沟）。他们无从知道自己的话竟被现实无情应验。去年，癌症的厄运又一次降临到我身上。这一次竟是我的两个乳房。我不得不做了双乳切除手术。

得知需要做手术的时候，我并没有把它当成什么大事。我甚至和朋友开玩笑说："我还会和你'齐胸并进'的"。毕竟，虽然我在 12 岁就因为癌症截了一条腿，但我仍然当上了滑雪世界冠军。我们这个滑雪队的队员们都有着这样或那样的肢体残缺。我见过一个男人，虽然坐着轮椅但却依然能

① prominent['prɔminənt] *adj.* 卓越的，显著的，突出的

② aggressive[ə'gresiv] *adj.* 好斗的，敢作敢为的，有闯劲的，侵略性的

③ slalom['sleiləm] *n.* 障碍滑雪

④ unique[juː'niːk] *adj.* 唯一的，独特的

够魅力十足,还有个女的,失去双手但却还像个正常人一样积极向上。很多事和肢体的残缺没有关系,关键在于勇气和精神。这些我都明白,但面对这些新的伤痕时,我吃惊地发现,要接受它们比登天还难。

从手术中苏醒过来,我泣不成声,胸口起伏难平。我突然意识到,我再也不愿看到自己的身体失去更多,我不想化疗,我不想再硬撑下去强颜欢笑。我希望自己永远不要醒来。我的呼吸开始变得微弱,麻醉师给我供氧,谢天谢地,不大一会儿我又昏昏睡去。

为了准备滑雪比赛,在做山地冲刺练习时,我的心脏、肺部以及腿部肌肉似乎要爆裂一般,有时我感觉体内的能量已被掏空,再也无法坚持下去。这时候我就会想到前方的比赛,想到自己挑战极限的梦想,想到突破自身障碍的满足,这些因素激励着我一次又一次地冲到了终点。坚韧不屈的竞赛精神同样帮助我第二次从癌症的阴影中走了出来。

乳房切除之后,我知道唯有重新投入锻炼才能让自己站起来,活下去。于是我前往本地的泳池。在公共淋浴间,我平生第一次注意到别人的乳房:D 罩的,A 罩的,下垂的,坚挺的。在失去一条腿之后这么多年,我突然第一次感觉到如此强烈的自卑,连脱衣服的勇气都没有了。

我决定要面对现实了,那天晚上,我在家里脱光衣服站在镜子前,长久审视着镜子中的自己。镜中的我难以分辨是男是女。我的脸孔,不化妆时分明是一个可爱的男孩子的脸。经常拄拐令我的肩膀、胳臂和双手强健有力。胸部没有了乳房,只剩下两个刺眼的伤疤。小腹平坦性感,臀部浑圆紧翘,大腿由于长期的滑雪运动变得健美挺拔。只是右腿仅剩膝以上的部分,留下一道长长的疤痕。

我发觉我很喜欢自己的这副身体,它很符合我的个性:既有男性的争强好胜,又有女性的温柔多情。因为平时我既喜欢戴着头盔、穿着防护服,挑战障碍滑雪的惊险刺激,又喜欢做着女人的春梦,比如生孩子,或者是打扮得漂漂亮亮,同情人共进晚餐,然后静静地靠在他身上,让他温柔地为自己除去衣衫。

后来我发现,胸部和腿部的疤痕其实对我影响深远。它们是我生命的印记。每一个人在生命中都会留下伤痕,只不过有些伤痕更加清晰。伤痕对于我们来说意义非凡,它们意味着生命,意味着我们没有逃避生活。当我们平和面对自己的伤痕,就会发现自身独有的美丽,就像那天我所做的一样。

再次去泳池的时候,在淋浴间,我已经可以坦然地同别人赤裸相对。

16. The Two Roads

It was New Year's Night. An aged man was standing at a window. He raised his mournful eyes towards the deep blue sky, where the stars were floating like white lilies on the surface of a clear calm lake. Then he cast them on the earth, where few more hopeless people than himself now moved towards their certain goal—the tomb. He had already passed sixty of the stages leading to it, and he had brought from his journey nothing but errors and remorse. Now his health was poor, his mind vacant, his heart sorrowful, and his old age short of comforts.

The days of his youth appeared like dreams before him, and he recalled the serious moment when his father placed him at the entrance of the two roads—one leading to a peaceful, sunny place, covered with flowers, fruits and resounding with soft, sweet songs; the other leading to a deep, dark cave, which was endless, where poison flowed instead of water and where devils and poisonous snakes hissed and crawled.

He looked towards the sky and cried painfully, "O youth, return! O my father, place me once more at the entrance to life, and I'll choose the better way!" But both his father and the days of his youth had passed away.

He saw the lights flowing away in the darkness. These were the days of his wasted life; he saw a star fall from the sky and disappeared, and this was the symbol of himself. His remorse, which was like a sharp arrow, struck deeply into his heart. Then he remembered his friends in his childhood, who entered on life together with him. But they had made their way to success and were now honoured and happy on this New Year's night.

The clock in the high church tower struck and the sound made him remember his parents' early love for him. They had taught him and prayed to God for his good. But he chose the wrong way. With shame and grief he dared no longer look towards that heaven where his father lives. His darkened eyes were full of tears, and with a despairing effort, he burst out a cry: "Come back, my early days! Come back!"

And his youth did return, for all this was only a dream which he had on New Year's Night. He was still young though his faults were real; he had not yet entered the deep, dark cave, and he was still free to walk on the road which leads to the peaceful and sunny land.

Those who still linger on the entrance of life, hesitating to choose the bright road, remember that when years are passed and your feet stumble on the dark mountains, you will cry bitterly, but in vain: "O youth, return! Oh give me back my early days!"

两 条 路

除夕之夜，一位老人伫立窗前。他满眼哀伤，仰望着深蓝色的天空，那儿，星星如清澈平静的湖面上的朵朵白莲在漂移着；后来，他将目光投向地面，几个比他更加绝望的人正在走向人生的终点——坟墓。在通往人生终点的道路上，他已走过了 60 多个驿站，除了过失和悔恨，他一无所获。现在，他健康欠佳，精神空虚，心情忧郁，缺少晚年应有的舒适和安逸。

青春的岁月如梦幻般浮现在他眼前，他回想起父亲将他放在人生岔路口上的关键时刻，当时，他面前有两条路：一条通向和平宁静、阳光灿烂的地方，那里到处是花果，到处回荡着柔和甜美的歌声；另一条则通向黑暗无底的深渊，那里流淌着毒液而不是清水，恶魔肆虐，毒蛇嘶嘶爬动。

他仰望天空，痛苦地哭喊："哦，青春，你回来吧！哦，爸爸，请把我重新放到人生的路口上吧，我会做出更好的选择。"然而他的父亲和他的青春年华皆离他远去。

他看见灯消逝在黑暗中，那便是他虚度的时光；他看见一颗星星从空中陨落、消失，那是他自身的象征。悔恨如同一支利箭，深深地刺进他的心。接着，他想起童年时代的朋友，他们曾与他一同踏上人生的旅程，现已获得成功，受到人们的尊敬，此刻正在幸福中欢度除夕。

教堂塔顶的钟声响了,使他回忆起父母早年对他的爱,他们曾给予他谆谆教诲,曾为他的幸福祈祷上帝。可他偏偏选择人生的歧途。羞愧和忧伤使他再也不敢正视他父亲所在的天堂。他双眼黯然无光,饱噙着泪水,在绝望中,他拼力高喊:“回来吧,我那逝去的年华!回来吧!”

青春真的回来了,因为以上所发生的一切只是他在除夕所做的一场梦。他仍旧年轻,当然他真的犯有过失,但还未坠入深渊;他仍然可以自由地走上通向宁静和光明的道路。

在人生路口徘徊,不知该不该选择光明大道的年轻人啊,你们千万要记住:当你青春已逝,双足在黑暗的群山中举步维艰、跌跌撞撞之时,你才痛心疾首地呼唤:“哦,回来吧,青春!哦,把我的美好年华还给我!”这只会是徒劳无益的。

17. Life Is All about Choices

Michael is the kind of guy you love to hate. He is always in a good mood and always has something positive to say. When someone would ask him how he was doing, he would reply, "If I were any better, I'd be twins!" He was a natural motivator.

If an employee was having a bad day, Michael was there telling the employee how to look on the positive side of the situation. Seeing this style really made me curious, so one day I went up to Michael and asked him, "I don't get it. You can't be positive all the time. How do you do it?"

Michael replied, "Each morning I wake up and say to myself 'Mike, you have two choices today. You can choose to be in a good mood or you can choose to be in a bad mood.' I choose to be in a good mood. Each time something bad happens, I can choose to be a victim① or choose to learn from it. I choose to learn from it. Every time someone comes to me complaining I can choose to accept their complaining or I can point out the positive② side of life. I choose the positive side of life."

"Yeah, right. It isn't that easy." I protested.

"Yes it is," Michael said. "Life is all about choices. When you cut away all the junk, every situation is a choice. You choose how you react to situations. You choose how people will affect your mood. You choose to be in a good mood or bad mood. The bottom line is: It's your choice how you live life." I reflected on what Michael said.

Soon thereafter, I left the big enterprise that I had worked in for years to start my own business. We lost touch, but I often thought about

① victim[ˈviktim] *n.* 受害人,牺牲者,牺牲品

② positive[ˈpɔzətiv] *adj.* 积极的

him when I made a choice about life instead of reacting to it. Several years later,I heard Michael was involved in a serious accident,falling off 60 feet from a communications tower.

After 18 hours of surgery,and weeks of intensive care,Michael was released from the hospital with rods placed in his back. I saw Michael about six months after the accident. When I asked him how he was,he replied,“If I were any better,I'd be twins. Wanna see my scars?”I declined to see his wounds,but did ask him what had gone through his mind as the accident took place.

“The first thing that went through my mind was the well being of my soon-to-be-born daughter,” Michael replied. “Then, as I lay on the ground,remembered I had two choices:I could choose to live or I could choose to die. I chose to live.” “Weren't you scared? Did you lose consciousness?”I asked. Michael continued,“...the paramedics① were great. They kept telling me I was going to be fine. But when they wheeled me into the operation room and I saw the expressions on the faces of the doctors and nurses,I got really scared. In their eyes,I read ‘He's a dead man.’ I knew I needed to take action.” “What did you do?”I asked. “Well,there was a big burly nurse shouting questions at me,”said Michael. “She asked me if I was allergic② to anything. ‘Yes,’ I said. The doctors and nurses stopped working as they waited for my reply. I took a deep breath and yelled,‘Gravity.’Over their laughter,I told them,‘I'm choosing to live. Operate on me as if I am alive,not dead’.”

Michael lived,thanks to the skill of his doctors,but also because of his amazing attitude. I learned from him that every day we have a choice to live fully. Attitude is everything.

① paramedic[ˈpærəˌmedik] n. 护理人员

② allergic[əˈləːdʒik] adj. [医]过敏的,患过敏症的

生活就是选择

迈克尔是那种你真想恨一恨的家伙，他总是乐呵呵的，总是说些积极上进的话。如果有人问他近况如何，他会这样回答："如果我还能再好，我就双倍地好了！"他生来就会让人积极进取。

如果哪位雇员有天过得很糟糕，迈克尔会告诉他如何看待形势的积极一面。他的这种方式着实让我好奇，所以有一天我找到迈克尔问："我真弄不明白。你不可能总是那样积极乐观，你是如何做到这一点的？"

迈克尔回答说，"每天早晨醒来时我对自己说，'迈克，今天你有两种选择。你可以选择心情愉快，你也可以选择心情恶劣。'我选择心情愉快。每次什么不愉快的事情发生时，我可以选择成为一个牺牲品，也可以选择从中吸取教训，而我选择从中吸取教训。每次有什么人找我来抱怨，我可以选择接受他们的抱怨，也可以选择向他指出生活的积极面。我选择生活的积极面。"

"是的，不错。可并不那么容易呀。"我表示异议。

"其实很容易，"迈克尔说。"生活就是选择。从每一事物中剔除一切枝节后剩下的都是一种选择。你选择如何应付生活中的种种情形。你选择他人会怎样影响你的情绪。你选择是心情愉快还是心情恶劣。说到底：如何生活是你自己的选择。"我琢磨着迈克尔的这席话。

那以后不久，我离开了工作数年的大企业去创建自己的公司。我们失去了联系，但当我对生活做出一种选择而非对它做出反应时，我时常想起迈克尔。几年之后，我听说迈克尔遭遇一场恶性事故，从一座通讯大楼的60英尺高处掉了下来。

在经历了18个小时的手术和数周的精心护理之后，迈克尔出院了，背部装有金属杆。大约事故半年之后，我见到了迈克尔。当我问他怎么样时，他回答，"如果我还能再好，我就双倍地好了。想看看我的伤疤吗？"我拒绝看他的伤痕，但的确问了他事故发生时他是怎么想的。

"我首先想到的是我那即将出世的女儿的幸福生活，"迈克尔答道。"当时我躺在地上，我记起我有两种选择：我可以选择活着，也可以选择死。

我选择了活。”“你难道不害怕吗？你失去知觉了吗？”我问。迈克尔接着说，“……那些护理人员棒极了。他们不停地告诉我我会好的。但当他们把我推进手术室，我看到医生和护士脸上的表情时，我真是吓坏了。在他们的眼里，我读出了‘他是个死人’。我知道我应该采取行动。”“你采取了什么行动？”我问道。“有一位人高马大的护士大声冲我问问题，”迈克尔说。“她问我是否对什么过敏。‘是的，’我说。医生和护士都停下手中的活儿等我回答。我深吸一口气大声说出，‘万有引力。’他们的笑声未了，我告诉他们，‘我选择活着。把我当活人而不是死人来做手术。’”

迈克尔活了下来，这要感谢他那些医生的高明医术，但也要归功于他那令人赞叹的态度。我从他那里学到了我们每天都有机会充实地活着，关键是态度。

18. A Little Piece of Me

When he told me he was leaving I felt like a vase which has just smashed. There were pieces of me all over the tidy, tan tiles. He kept talking, telling me why he was leaving, explaining it was for the best, I could do better, it was his fault and not mine. I had heard it before many times and yet somehow was still not immune①; perhaps one did not become immune to such felony②.

He left and I tried to get on with my life. I filled the kettle and put it on to boil, I took out my old red mug and filled it with coffee watching as each coffee granule③ slipped into the bone china. That was what my life had been like, endless omissions of coffee granules, somehow never managing to make that cup of coffee.

Somehow when the kettle piped its finishing warning I pretended not to hear it. That's what Mike's leaving had been like, sudden and with an awful finality④. I would rather just wallow in uncertainty than have things finished. I laughed at myself. Imagine getting all philosophical and sentimental⑤ about a mug of coffee. I must be getting old.

And yet it was a young woman who stared back at me from the mirror. A young woman full of promise and hope, a young woman with bright eyes and full lips just waiting to take on the world. I never loved Mike anyway. Besides there are more important things. More important than love, I

① immune [i'mjuːn] *adj.* 免疫的
② felony ['feləni] *n.* [律]重罪
③ granule ['grænjuːl] *n.* 小粒,颗粒,细粒
④ finality [fai'næliti] *n.* 结尾,定局,终结
⑤ sentimental [ˌsenti'mentl] *adj.* 感伤性的,感情脆弱的

insist to myself firmly. The lid goes back on the coffee just like closure on the whole Mike experience.

He doesn't haunt my dreams as I feared that night. Instead I am flying far across fields and woods, looking down on those below me. Suddenly I fall to the ground and it is only when I wake up that I realize I was shot by a hunter, brought down by the burden of not the bullet but the soul of the man who shot it. I realize later, with some degree of understanding, that Mike was the hunter holding me down and I am the bird that longs to fly. The next night my dream is similar to the previous① night, but without the hunter. I fly free until I meet another bird who flies with me in perfect harmony. I realize with some relief that there is a bird out there for me, there is another person, not necessarily a lover perhaps just a friend, but there is someone out there who is my soul mate. I think about being a broken vase again and realize that I have glued myself back together, what Mike has is merely a little part of my time in earth, a little understanding of my physical being. He has only, a little piece of me.

我的一小片

当他告诉我他要离开的时候,我感觉自己就像花瓶被摔成了碎片,跌落在茶色瓷砖地板上。他一直在说话,解释着为什么要离开,说什么这是最好的,我可以做得更好,都是他的错,与我无关。虽然这些话以前听了许多遍,但无论如何都难免受伤,或许没有人能对如此大的打击无动于衷。

他走了,我努力过自己的生活。我往水壶里灌满水,放在炉子上烧开,拿出我那个红色的旧杯子,看着咖啡粉末一点点地落入骨瓷杯子里。这是我以前的生活,不断地加咖啡粉末,却从来没有真正地泡成一杯咖啡。

① previous[ˈpriːvjəs] *adj.* 在前的,早先的

水开了,水壶发出警报声,我假装没有听见。迈克的离去也是一样,突如其来,并且无可挽回。我宁愿活在朦朦胧胧之中,也不愿意看到事情的结局。我嘲笑自己,自己竟然为一杯咖啡有如此多的人生感怀,我自己一定是老了。

可是镜子里回望着我的那个女孩还是那么年轻啊!明眸皓齿,充满了前途与希望,光明的未来在向她招手。反正我也从来没有爱过迈克。何况,生命中还有比爱更重要的东西在等待着我,我对自己坚持说。我将咖啡罐的盖子盖好,也将所有关于迈克的记忆尘封起来。

那天晚上,他没有像我担心的那样进入我的梦中。在梦里,我飞过田野和森林,俯瞰着大地。突然间,我掉了下来……醒来后才发现原来自己被猎人打中了,但是令我坠落的不是他的子弹,而是他的灵魂。我后来才渐渐明白,原来迈克就是那个使我坠落的猎人,而我是那只渴望飞翔的小鸟。到了第二天晚上,我仍然做了类似的梦,但是猎人不见了,我一直在自由地飞翔,直到遇上另外一只小鸟和我比翼双飞。我开始意识到,总有那么一只鸟,那么一个人在前面等我,这个人不一定是我的爱人,也许只是个朋友,但一定是我灵魂的伴侣,这令我感觉如释重负。我想起曾经觉得自己像花瓶一样裂开了,才意识到原来自己已经把自己粘在一起了。迈克只是我生命的一小片,他仅仅了解我的表面,他仅仅是我生命中的小小一部分。

19. My Irreplaceable Treasure

Recently I gave a dinner party for some close friends. To add a touch of elegance① to the evening, I brought out the good stuff—my white Royal Crown Derby china with the fine blue-and-gold border. When we were seated, one of the guests noticed the beat-up gravy boat I'd placed among the newer, better dinnerware. "Is it an heirloom?" she asked tactfully.

I admit the piece does look rather conspicuous②. For one thing, it matches nothing else. It's also old and chipped. But that little gravy boat is much more than an heirloom③ to me. It is the one thing in this world I will never part with.

The story begins more than 50 years ago, when I was seven years old and we lived in a big house along the Ohio River in New Richmond, Ohio. All that separated the house from the river was the street and our wide front lawn. In anticipation④ of high water, the ground floor had been built seven feet above grade.

Late in December the heavy rains came, and the river climbed to the tops of its banks. When the water began to rise in a serious way, my parents made plans in case the river should invade⑤ our house. My mother decided she would pack our books and her fine china in a small den off the master bedroom.

The china was not nearly as good as it was old. Each piece had a gold rim and a band of roses. But the service had been her mother's and was precious to her. As she packed the china with great care, she said to me, "You must treasure the things that people you love have cherished. It

① elegance['eligəns] *n.* 高雅，典雅，优雅

② conspicuous[kən'spikjuəs] *adj.* 显著的

③ heirloom['eəluːm] *n.* 传家宝，相传动产

④ anticipation[ˌæntisi'peiʃən] *n.* 预期，预料

⑤ invade[in'veid] *v.* 侵略，侵袭

keeps you in touch with them."

I didn't understand, since I'd never owned① anything I cared all that much about. Still, planning for disaster held considerable② fascination for me.

The plan was to move upstairs if the river reached the seventh of the steps that led to the front porch. We would keep a rowboat downstairs so we could get from room to room. The one thing we would not do was leave the house. My father, the town's only doctor, had to be where sick people could find him.

I checked on the river's rise several times a day and lived in a state of hopeful alarm that the water would climb all the way up to the house. It did not disappoint. The muddy water rose higher until, at last, the critical seventh step was reached.

We worked for days carrying things upstairs, until, late one afternoon, the water edged over the threshold③ and rushed into the house. I watched, amazed at how rapidly it rose.

After the water got about a foot deep inside the house, it was hard to sleep at night. The sound of the river moving about downstairs was frightening. Debris had broken windows, so every once in a while some floating battering ram—a log or perhaps a table—would bang into the walls and make a sound like a distant drum.

Every day I sat on the landing and watched the river rise. Mother cooked simple meals in a spare bedroom she had turned into a makeshift kitchen. She was worried, I could tell, about what would happen to us. Father came and went in a small fishing boat. He was concerned about his patients and possible outbreaks of dysentery, pneumonia④ or typhoid.

Before long, the Red Cross began to pitch tents on high ground north of town. "We are staying right here," my father said.

① own[əun] v. 拥有,自认,承认
② considerable[kən'sidərəbl] adj. 相当大(或多)的,值得考虑的,相当可观的
③ threshold['θreʃhəuld] n. 门槛
④ pneumonia[nju(:)'məunjə] n. [医] 肺炎

As the water continued to rise, I kept busy rowing through the house and looking at the furniture that had been too big to move upstairs. I liked to row around the great cozy① couch, now almost submerged, and pretend it was an island in a lake.

One night very late I was awakened by a tearing noise, like timbers creaking. Then there was the rumbling sound of heavy things falling. I jumped out of bed and ran into the hallway. My parents were standing in the doorway to the den, where we had stored the books and my mother's beloved china.

The floor of the den had fallen through, and all the treasures we had tried to save were now on the first floor, under the stealthily② rising river. My father lit our camp light, and we went to the landing to look. We could see nothing except the books bobbing like little rafts on the water.

Mother had been courageous, it seemed to me, through the ordeal of the flood. She was steady and calm, and kept things going in good order. But that night she sat on the top of the stairs with her head on her crossed arms and cried. I had never seen her like that, and there was a sound in her weeping that made me afraid. I wanted to help her, but I couldn't think of what I could possibly do. I just knew I had to figure out something.

The next morning, after breakfast, I did a geography lesson and then Mother said I could go downstairs and play in the boat. I rowed once around the downstairs, avoiding the mess of timbers in the hall where the terrible accident had occurred. The books had begun to sink. I stared down into the dark water and could see nothing. It was right then that I got the idea.

I made a hook from a wire coathanger③ and carefully fastened it to a weighted line . Then I let it sink and began to drag it slowly back and

① cozy['kəuzi] *adj.* 舒适的，安逸的，惬意的

② stealthily['steləili] *adv.* 暗地里，悄悄地

③ coathanger['kəuthæŋə] *n.* 衣架

forth①. I spent the next hour or so moving the boat and dragging my line—hoping to find pieces of my mother's lost treasure. But time after time the line came up empty.

As the water rose day after day, I continued trying to recover some remnant② of my mother's broken china. Soon, however, the water inside had risen to the stairway landing. On the day water covered the gutters outside, my father decided we would have to seek shelter in the tents on the hill. A powerboat was to pick us up that afternoon. We would leave by the porch roof.

I spent the morning hurriedly securing things in my room. Then I got into my rowboat③ for the last time. I dragged my line through the water. Nothing. After some time I heard my parents calling, so I headed back toward the stairway. Just as I made the last turn, I snagged something.

Holding my breath, I slowly raised my catch to the surface. As the dark water drained from it, I could make out the bright roses and gold leaf design. It seemed dazzling to me. I had found the gravy boat from my mother's china service. My line had caught on a small chip in the lip.

My father called down to me again. "This is serious business," he said. "Let's go." So I stowed the treasure in my jacket and rowed as fast as I could to the stair landing.

The powerboat picked us up and headed to higher ground. It began to rain, and for the first time I was really afraid. The water might rise forever, might cover the whole valley, the trees, even the hills.

By the time we were settled in a Red Cross tent, we were worn out. Father had gone off to care for sick people, and

① back and forth 来来往往地,来回地
② remnant[ˈremnənt] *n.* 残余,剩余,零料,残迹
③ rowboat[ˈrəubəut] *n.* 划艇,小舟

Mother sat on my cot① with her arm around my shoulder. She smiled at me, if you can call it that. Then I reached under my pillow and took out the gravy boat.

She looked at it, then at me. Then she took it in her hands and held it for a long time. She was very quiet, just sitting, gazing at the gravy boat. She seemed both close to me and also very far away, as though she was remembering. I don't know what she was thinking, but she pulled me into her arms and held me tight.

We lived in the tent for weeks, cold and often hungry. As the flood crested, an oil slick caught fire and burned our house down to the waterline. We never went back. Instead, we moved to a house near Cincinnati, far from the river.

By Easter we were settled in, and we celebrated that special Sunday with a feast. While Dad carved the lamb, Mother went into the kitchen and returned with the gravy boat. She held my gift for a moment as though it was something unspeakably precious. Then, smiling at me, she placed it gently on the table. I said to myself right then that nothing would ever happen to that gravy boat as long as I lived.

And nothing ever has. Now I use the gravy boat just as she had, taking it carefully from the shelf and filling it just as she did with dark, rich turkey gravy for family dinners and other special occasions. When guests ask about the curious old dish, I sometimes tell the story of how I fished it from the river in our house.

But beyond the events of the flood, the gravy② boat is a treasure that connects me to the people and the places of my past. Mother tried to explain, and now I understand. It is not the object so much as

① cot[kɔt] n. 轻便小床，帆布床

② gravy['greivi] n. 肉汁，肉汤

the connection that I cherish①. That little porcelain② boat, chipped and worn with age, keeps me in touch—just as she said it would—with her life, her joy and her love.

我无可替代的珍宝

最近我举办了一次宴会,招待几位好友。为了给那个晚上增添一点雅致,我摆出了一件好东西——绘有精美蓝边和金边的白色王冠德比牌的瓷器。大伙儿就座后,其中一位客人注意到了这只残破的船形深底盘——我已把它放在了更新更好的餐具当中。“这是一件传家宝吗?”她机敏地问道。

我承认这只盘子看起来确实惹人注目。首先,它跟其他任何东西都不相匹配;再者,它古旧而且有缺口。但对我而言,这只小小的船形深底盘不只是一件传家宝。它是这个世界上我一生都不会放弃的珍爱之物。

故事发生在50多年前,当时我才7岁,我们家住在俄亥俄州新里士满俄亥俄河边的一幢大房子里。房子跟河水只隔着一条街道和房前宽阔的草坪。考虑到河水有上涨的可能,房子一楼的地板安装得比地面高出7英尺。

12月下旬下起了大暴雨,河水涨到河沿上。河水刚开始猛涨时,我爸妈就作出了各种方案,以防河水淹进我们的房子。妈妈决定将我们所有的书籍以及她的精美瓷器搬出大卧室,放在楼上的小书斋里。

这些瓷器丝毫也显不出年代久远的痕迹。每一件都绘有金边和玫瑰花束。这套餐具是我外婆遗留下来的,对我妈来说十分珍贵。她一边小心翼翼地把它们包好,一边对我说:“你必须珍惜这些你所爱的人曾经珍惜过的东西。这可以保持你同它们的联系。”

我当时并不懂得她的意思,因为我从未拥有过什么能令我如此珍爱的东西。不过,为了防备遭受灾难而出谋划策使我兴趣盎然。

家里的计划是,如果河水上涨到通向前廊的第七级台阶,我们就搬到楼上去。我们将在楼下系一条划艇,以便能够从一个房间划到另

① cherish[ˈtʃeriʃ]v. 珍爱,怀抱

② porcelain[ˈpɔːslin]n. & adj. 瓷器;瓷制的,精美的

一个房间。我们就是不愿意离开自己的家园。我爸爸是镇上唯一的一名大夫，他得守在病人能找到他的地方。

我每天查看几次河水上涨的情况，并惊恐地预料河水会一直漫进屋里。果然不出所料，浑浊的河水竟不断地高涨，终于淹到了至关重要的第七级台阶。

连着几天，我们忙于把东西搬到楼上，有一天一直忙到下午五六点钟，河水徐徐地漫过门槛，冲进屋里。我监视着，发现河水上涨的速度快得令人惊讶。

当屋里的积水深达一英尺时，晚上就很难睡个安稳觉了。河水在楼下撞击的声音叫人惊恐万分。随水冲进来的碎石片击碎了窗户玻璃，偶尔，飘浮在水上的撞击物——一根圆木，也有可能是一张桌子——会猛烈地撞到墙上，发出的声音像是远方传来的鼓声。

每天我都坐在楼梯平台上，看着河水上涨。妈妈把楼上一间空余的卧室临时当作厨房，做一些简单的饭菜。我看得出来，她对我们将要面临的困境深感忧虑。爸爸坐在一条小渔船上来来去去。他担心的是他的病人以及可能突然蔓延开来的痢疾、肺炎和伤寒等诸多疾病。

不久，红十字会开始在小镇北面的高地上架设帐篷。“我们就待在家里，”爸爸说。

河水继续上涨，我不停地划着船，在屋里来回穿梭，看一看那些没法搬上楼去的大件家具。我喜欢划到那张舒适的长沙发椅的四周转悠，如今它差不多浸在了水下，我把它设想成一座湖心岛。

一天深夜，我被一阵猛烈撕扯的声音惊醒，好像是木头在吱吱嘎嘎地断裂。然后传来重物坍塌时的隆隆声。我跳下床，冲进过道。爸妈正站在小书斋的门口，小书斋里存放着全家人的书籍和妈妈珍爱的那套瓷器。

小书斋的地板已经塌陷下去，我们一直设法保全的珍贵瓷器如今都落到楼下的地板上了，淹没在不停暗涨的河水里。爸爸点亮露营用的灯，我们借着灯光到楼梯平台上察看。除了书籍像小木筏一样飘浮在水面上，什么也看不见。

在我看来，妈妈一直勇敢地经受着这场洪水的严峻考验。她从容、镇静，把每一件事情都安排得有条不紊。可是那个晚上，她坐在楼梯口上抱头痛哭。我以前从未见过她这般伤心,她的哭声让我感到有些害怕。我想帮她,却又不知所措。我只知道我必须把什么事情弄清楚。

第二天上午吃过早餐,我做完地理功课,妈妈说我可以下楼到船上去玩了。我在楼下划了一圈,绕开门厅头天晚上掉下来的乱七八糟的木料。水面上的书籍已经开始下沉。我盯着黑漆漆的水往下瞧,什么也看不见,就在这个时候我计上心来。

我用金属衣架做了一个钩子,小心翼翼地把它系到一根加重的绳子上。接着我将它沉入水中,开始缓慢地来回拖动。我花了大约一个小时,划船,拖绳——希望能够找到妈妈失去的那套珍贵的瓷器。但一次又一次,绳子拉上来,空无一物。

河水日复一日地涨个不停,我继续尝试着去找回妈妈的哪怕是一些已经破损的瓷器的残片。可是不多时,楼下的河水已涨到了楼梯平台上。河水淹上房外檐槽的那一天,爸爸决定,我们必须到山上的帐篷里寻求庇护了。当天下午有一艘汽艇来接我们,我们将从前廊的屋顶上撤离。

我上午匆匆忙忙地将我房间里的东西捆牢。然后我跳上划艇准备作最后一次努力。我把绳子拖过水面。什么也没有。过了一会儿,听到爸妈在叫,我只好朝着楼梯的方向往回划。就在我转最后一个弯时,我钩住了什么东西。

我屏住呼吸,慢慢地将打捞到的物品拉上水面。它刚一浮出黑色的河水,我就辨认出鲜亮的玫瑰以及金色的花瓣图案。我感到一阵晕眩。我竟然找到了妈妈那套瓷器中的这只船形深底盘。我的绳子刚好挂住了这只瓷盘边上的一个小缺口。

爸爸又在朝下喊我。"这可不是闹着玩的,"他说。"咱们快走。"我便把这件宝物藏在上衣里,尽快地朝楼梯平台划过去。

汽艇带上我们往高地方向驶去。天又开始下雨,我第一次真正感到了害怕。河水也许会涨个没完,淹没整个山谷、树林甚至山丘。

我们在红十字会的帐篷里安顿下来,全都精疲力竭。爸爸照看病人去了;妈妈坐在我的帆布床上,搂着我的肩头。她对着我微笑——如果那能称为微笑的话。这当儿,我把手伸到枕头下面,拿出了那只船形深底盘。

她先看了看盘子,然后看着我。接着她把盘子拿过去握了很久。她十分平静，就那样坐着，凝视着这件珍品。她离我很近，却又仿佛非常遥远，好像陷入了某种回忆。我不知道她在想什么，但她将我拥入怀里，紧紧地抱着。

我们在帐篷里住了几个星期，常常忍饥耐寒。洪峰到来时，水面上的一层油膜不幸着火，把我家的房子吃水线以上部分全部烧塌。我们再也没有回去，而是举家迁往离河很远的辛辛那提附近的另一幢房子。

复活节那天，我们住进了新家，举行盛宴庆祝那个特别的星期日。趁爸爸在切羊肉，妈妈走进厨房拿出那只船形深底盘。好一阵子，她捧着我的这份礼物，仿佛这是一件无法用言语形容的最宝贵的器皿。然后，她一边微笑着望着我，一边轻轻地将盘子放到餐桌上。就在那时我对自己说，只要我活着，我决不会再让这只盘子出事。

的确一直没有出事。如今我就像妈妈当年一样使用着这只盘子，小心翼翼地从碗柜的隔板上拿下来，在家庭晚宴上和其他特别的节日里盛上黑色而肥美的火鸡肉汁。当有客人问起这只奇特而古老的盘子时，我偶尔也会讲讲这个故事，告诉他们我是如何从淹入我家的河水里捞出来的。

但是除了那场洪水的经历之外，这只船形深底盘还是一件将我同我过去的亲人和住处紧密相连的珍奇之物。妈妈曾努力解释过这一点，如今我真正感悟到了。我珍惜的与其说是这件器皿本身，还不如说是通过它而建立起来的那种联系。这只小小的船形瓷器，年深日久，伤痕累累，却将我同妈妈的人生、妈妈的欢乐和妈妈的慈爱永远相连——正如她曾经说过的那样。

20. Paradox of Our Times

We have bigger houses and smaller families; more conveniences①, but less time; we have more degrees, but less common sense②; more knowledge, but less judgment; more experts, but more problems; more medicine, but less wellness.

We spend too recklessly, laugh too little, drive too fast, get to angry too quickly, stay up too late, get up too tired, read too little, watch TV too often, and pray too seldom.

We have multiplied③ our possessions④, but reduced our values. We talk too much, love too little and lie too often. We've learned how to make a living, but not a life; we've added years to life, not life to years.

We have taller buildings, but shorter tempers; wider freeways, but narrower viewpoints. We spend more, but have less; we buy more, but enjoy it less.

We've been all the way to the moon and back, but have trouble crossing the street to meet the new neighbor. We've conquered outer space, but not inner space. We've split the atom, but not our prejudice⑤; we write more, but learn less; plan more, but accomplish less.

We've learned to rush, but not to wait; we have higher incomes, but lower morals⑥. We build more computers to hold more information, to produce more copies, but have less communication. We are long on quantity, but short on quality.

These are the times of fast foods and slow digestion⑦; tall men and

---

① convenience[kən'viːnjəns] n. 便利,方便
② common sense n. 常识(尤指判断力)
③ multiply['mʌltiplai] v. 繁殖,乘,增加
④ possession[pə'zeʃən] n. 拥有物,占有物
⑤ prejudice['predʒudis] n. 偏见,成见
⑥ morals['mɔrəlz] n. 道德
⑦ digestion[di'dʒestʃən] n. 消化力

short character; steep① profits and shallow relationships. More leisure and less fun; more kinds of food, but less nutrition②; two incomes, but more divorce; fancier houses, but broken homes.

我们这个时代的尴尬

我们的房屋在扩大，家庭却在缩小；生活越来越便利，时间却越来越少；学位证书越拿越多，基本常识却愈加匮乏；知识越来越丰富，判断力却日趋迟钝；专家越来越多，问题却也日益增加；药物越吃越多，健康却每况愈下。

我们花钱太鲁莽，笑容太少，车开得太快，太容易动怒，熬夜太晚，起床时太累，书读得太少，电视看得太勤，祷告做得太少。

我们不断聚敛物质财富，却逐渐丢失了自我价值。我们说得太多，爱得太少，谎言泛滥。我们掌握了谋生手段，却不懂得生活真谛；我们不断地延年益寿，却没有为生命注入活力。

我们的房子越住越高，脾气却越来越糟；我们行驶的道路越来越宽阔，眼光却越来越狭隘。我们付出很多，可获得的很少；我们购买了很多，可从中得到的乐趣却很少。

我们能够往返于地球与月球之间，却不乐于穿过马路向新邻居问好。我们已经征服太空，却无法逾越内心的沟鸿；我们已经让原子分裂，却不能突破思想偏见；我们写的很多，可学到的很少；计划很多，可完成的很少。

我们学会了追赶时间，却没学会耐心等待；我们拥有的财富越来越多，道德品质却日益沦丧。我们生产更多的电脑用于存储更多的信息和制造更多的拷贝，而相互间的交流与沟通却越来越少。我们渴求数量，却忽视质量。

这是一个快餐食品与消化迟缓相伴的时代；一个体格高大和性格病态并存的时代；一个追名逐利和人情冷漠相生的时代。我们的休闲多了，乐趣却少了；食品种类多了，营养却少了；双薪家庭增加了，离婚率也激升了；居室的装修华丽了，家庭却残缺破碎了。

① steep[stiːp] *adj.* 急剧升降的

② nutrition[njuːˈtriʃən] *n.* 营养，营养学

21. The Important Things in Life

Sometimes people come into your life and you know right away that they were meant to be there, to serve some sort of purpose, teach you a lesson, or to help you figure out who you are or who you want to become.

You never know who these people may be—a roommate, a neighbor, a professor, a friend, a lover, or even a complete stranger—but when you lock eyes with them, you know at that very moment they will affect your life in some profound① way.

Sometimes things happen to you that may seem horrible, painful, and unfair at first, but in reflection you find that without overcoming those obstacles you would have never realized your potential, strength, willpower, or heart.

Illness, injury, love, lost moments of true greatness, and sheer stupidity② all occur to test the limits of your soul. Without these small tests, whatever they may be, life would be like a smoothly paved straight flat road to nowhere. It would be safe and comfortable, but dull and utterly③ pointless.

The people you meet who affect your life, and the success and downfalls you experience, help to create who you are and who you become. Even the bad experiences can be learned from. In fact, they are sometimes the most important ones.

If someone loves you, give love back to them in whatever way you can, not only because they love you, but because in a way, they are teaching you to love and how to open your heart and eyes to things.

If someone hurts you, betrays you, or breaks your heart, forgive them , for they have helped you learn about trust and the importance of

① profound[prə'faund] *adj.* 深刻的,意义深远的

② stupidity[stju(:)'piditi] *n.* 愚蠢,糊涂事

③ utterly['ʌtəli] *adv.* 完全地,绝对地,彻底地

being cautious[①] to whom you open your heart.

Make every day count. Appreciate every moment and take from those moments everything that you possibly can for you may never be able to experience it again. Talk to people that you have never talked to before, and listen to what they have to say.

Let yourself fall in love, break free, and set your sights high. Hold your head up because you have every right to. Tell yourself you are a great individual and believe in yourself, for if you don't believe in yourself, it will be hard for others to believe in you.

You can make anything you wish of your life. Create your own life and then go out and live it with absolutely no regrets.

And if you love someone tell them, for you never know what tomorrow may have in store.

一生中要紧的事

有时,一旦有人走入你的生命,你就会立即明白他们本来就在那里,要么达成某种目的,给予你处事的道理,要么帮你认清你自己,要么帮你实现理想。

你永远不知道这些人会是谁——一位室友,一位邻居,一位教授,一位友人,一位情人或者是位陌生人——然而,当你闭上眼睛想起他们时,那一刻,你会明白他们在某些方面深深地影响着你的生活。

有时,发生在你身上的事情首先看起来有点可怕,有点痛苦还有点不公,而你反省之后,你会发现不克服这些障碍,你永远也意识不到自己的潜力、实力、毅力还有心地。

疾病,伤害,爱情,那些逝去的真正伟大时刻,以及种种愚蠢行为都可以验证你灵魂的底线。无论这些小小的测验是什么,没有它们,生活就会像一个平坦的大道,伸向没有终极的目标。它可能安全舒适,却乏味枯燥,完全

① cautious[ˈkɔːʃəs] *adj.* 谨慎的,小心的

没有意义。

在你的人生中，那些你遇见过的影响你生活的人，以及你所经历的大起大落，都会帮你创造自己，实现自己。你甚至可以从那些糟糕的经历中学到东西。实际上，它们有时会成为你人生中最重要的经历。

如若有人爱你，无论你用何种方式，一定要投桃报李；不仅仅因为他们爱你，而是因为他们教你怎样去爱，怎样敞开你的心扉，开阔你的视野。

如若有人伤害了你，背叛了你，或者伤了你的心，原谅他们，因为他们帮你学会了信任，学会了对一个人敞开心扉时要谨慎小心。

让每一天都有价值，珍惜每一刻，尽可能从那些时光中有所收获，因为这些经历你可能不会再次重复。和那些你往日没有讲过话的人交流，听听他们的心声。

让你自己陷入爱的漩涡之后从中解脱，然后放远眼光。你应该昂头挺胸，对自己充满信心，因为你有权利这样做。要从内心告诉自己你是一位了不起的人，并相信自己，如若你自己不相信自己，也很难让其他人来信任你。

你可以按照自己的愿望计划生活。创造你自己的人生，按照你设计的方式毫无遗憾地度过。

你如若爱上某个人，就告诉他（她），因为你永远不会知道明天等待你的会是什么。

22. Harder to Be Kind than Clever

As a kid, I spent my summers with my grandparents on their ranch in Cotulla, Texas. I helped fix windmills①, vaccinate② cattle and did other ranch chores. It was hard work but a welcome change from my Houston life of school and playing Star Trek with my friends. I loved it.

One of the best and strangest parts of spending summers with my grandparents was caravanning③ with Wally Bryam Caravan Club, a group of Airstream trailer owners who took road trips together around the United States and Canada. My grandparents were members and owned a thirty-one-foot Airstream that they towed behind their 1973 Oldsmobile. Every few summers, we would join the caravan line of some three hundred Airstream trailers, and it was during one these trips that my grandfather said to me the right words at the right time.

I wasn't very old, maybe ten or eleven, but I was forming my opinions about the world, and, of course, I thought I knew much more about things than I actually did.

I was then, as I am now, a big reader and a fiend for numbers. Anyone who has been on a long road trip knows that no matter how many books you bring, no matter how sparkling④ the conversation or beautiful the scenery, you still have too much time to think. So I spent a good deal of my extra time calculating. I calculated gas mileage⑤. I

---

① windmill['windmil] *n.* 风车

② vaccinate['væksineit] *v.* 进行预防接种

③ caravan['kærəvæn] *v.* 乘宿营旅行车度假

④ sparkling ['spɑːkliŋ] *adj.* 闪烁的,闪闪发光的,发泡的

⑤ mileage['mailidʒ] *n.* 英里数,英里里程

figured out the average per-item price of groceries bought over the course of the trip. And at some point, I saw an antismoking ad on TV. The announcer declared that every time a smoker took a puff ①of cigarette, he was shortening his life span by two minutes. My grandmother was a smoker. I hated it, and not just because I knew that it was bad for her. My guess is that any kid who rides for thousands of miles sitting in the smoke-filled backseat of a 1973 Oldsmobile grows to hate smoking. So on one particularly long driving day, I decided to do the math.

I don't remember exactly what the number was —two minutes per puff, twenty puffs per cigarette, twenty cigarettes per pack, one pack a day for thirty years. About sixteen years? When I was satisfied that I had come up with a reasonably accurate② number, I poked my head between the two front seats and tapped my grandmother on the shoulder. "You've taken sixteen years off your life from smoking," I said, explaining the math, and with none of the solemnity③ the disclosure warranted④. She burst into tears.

It was not the "You're very clever—that's good math" reaction that I was expecting. But there's nothing like unintentionally stepping on a landmine to make you keenly aware of your effect on those around you. I felt terrible. I sat quietly in the backseat unsure of what to do.

My grandmother cried, and my grandfather, who had been driving in silence, carefully pulled to the side of the road. He got out of the car and asked me to follow. Was I in trouble? How much trouble was I in? My grandfather has never said a harsh word to me, but this incident was unprecedented. I had no way to gauge⑤ how severe the consequences would be.

We walked a few paces back and stood between the trunk of the car

① puff[pʌf] *n.* 包,盒

② accurate['ækjurit] *adj.* 正确的,精确的

③ solemnity[sə'lemniti] *n.* 严肃,一本正经

④ warrant['wɔrənt] *v.* 保证,辩解,担保

⑤ gauge[geidʒ] *v.* 测量,测定

and the front of the silver trailer. I watched the parade of Airstream trailers drive by and waited for the rebuke① I knew was coming. After a minute, my grandfather looked at me, put his hand on my shoulder and said: "You'll learn one day that it's much harder to be kind than clever."

With both his words and the gentle way in which he delivered them, my grandfather taught me an essential② lesson. I had always admired him for his intelligence③, but that day I began to understand that his intelligence was only a gift that he had been given. It was the kindness with which he chose to apply it that he could be proud of. It's something I've been working on ever since.

聪明难，善良更难

小时候，我的夏天是与祖父母一起在得克萨斯州的可图拉农场度过的。我帮助修风车，给牛接种疫苗，干了好多农场上的杂活儿。农场上的活儿很辛苦，但相对于我在休斯敦度过的学校时光以及同朋友一起玩星际旅行游戏的那种生活而言，农场生活是一种让人高兴的改变。我喜欢农场上的生活。

在与祖父母一起度过的夏天生活中最有意思、最为奇特的部分便是和瓦立·布莱姆房车国际俱乐部一起旅行。该俱乐部的成员都是"气流"房车的车主，他们开车绕美国和加拿大旅行。我的祖父母也是该俱乐部的成员，他们拥有一辆31英尺的"气流"房车，就拖在他们的那辆1973年的奥兹莫比尔老式汽车后面。每隔几个夏天，我们便加入车队——通常有300多辆"气流"房车——参加旅行。正是在这些旅途中，祖父在恰当的时候对我说了许多中肯的话。

那时候我的年纪不大，也就10岁或11岁的样子，但却正处在世界观形成的时候。当然，我总是认为自己懂得很多，虽然事实并非如此。

那时候的我和现在一样，热爱读书并且对数学很着迷。经历过长途旅行的人都知道，在旅途中无论你准备多少书，无论旅途中的谈话多么精彩，

① rebuke[riˈbjuːk] *v.* 斥责，指责，非难

② essential[iˈsenʃəl] *adj.* 本质的，实质的，基本的

③ intelligence[inˈtelidʒəns] *n.* 智力，聪明，智能

也无论旅途中的景色多么漂亮,你总有太多的时间来思考。所以我的大部分时间都用来计算了。我计算油费,计算在旅途中购买的每一样东西的平均价格。有一次,我还看了一则电视上的禁烟广告。广告里说吸烟者每吸一口烟,寿命就会缩短2分钟。祖母就是个烟民。我很讨厌她吸烟,原因当然不只是因为我知道吸烟对她的健康有害,还因为我猜想任何一个小孩坐在烟雾缭绕的1973年的奥兹默比尔老式汽车后座上行驶成千上万英里都会逐渐地讨厌吸烟。所以在某一个长时间坐车的日子,我决定好好算算有关吸烟与寿命减短的这道题。

我现在已经记不清具体的数字了——1口烟缩短寿命2分钟,一根烟吸20口,一盒烟有20根,30年里每天一盒烟。祖母的吸烟量算下来好像对应的是缩短寿命16年吧?当我对自己算出的相对准确的数字感到满意时,我将头伸到前排的两个座位之间,拍了拍祖母的肩膀说,"因为吸烟,你会少活16年。"我一边说,一边解释这个数字是怎么算出来的,并没在意这句话将会带来的后果。祖母听完后哭了。

大家的反应并不是我所期待的称赞"这孩子真聪明——这道算术题算得不错"。这件事并不像你无意中踩上地雷,后果怎样你会清楚地明了。我觉得挺可怕的,于是安静地坐在后排座位上,不知道该做什么。

祖母哭了,一直静静地在开车的祖父小心地将车停到了路边,他下了车,并且让我也下车。我闯祸了吗?我闯了多大的祸?在此之前,祖父从来未对我说过一句重话。但这次的事以前从未发生过。我无法预料这次后果会有多么严重。

我和祖父往后走了几步,在老汽车的后备箱和后拖的银色房车之间的位置站住了。我一边看着"气流"房车车队的通过,一边等着祖父的责备。过了一分钟,祖父看着我,用手拍着我的肩膀说:"孩子,有一天你会明白,聪明难,善良更难。"

祖父的话和他那种轻轻的说话方式给我上了重要的一课。一直以来我很崇拜祖父的智慧,但在那一天我开始认识到祖父的智慧不过是上天赐给他的一种禀赋,而他选择通过善良来运用这种禀赋的做法才是他真正值得骄傲和自豪的。而从那时起,我便一直朝着这个方向努力。

23. The Gift

It was well after midnight, wrapped in my warm fleecy[1] robe I stood silently staring out the ninth floor window of the daunting New York Hospital. I was staring at the 59th Street Bridge. It was as sparkling and beautiful as a Christmas tree. New York City has always been special to me; the Broadway theatre, the music, the restaurants from the deli's[2] to the Tavern[3]-on-the-Green. "This is what the city is supposed to be about," I thought, dreading the morning to come and all the uncertainty it held. But the morning did come and at nine a. m. on that March 17th, I was wheeled into an operating room. Eleven hours and forty-five minutes later I was wheeled into a recovery room and a very few hours after being returned to my own hospital room I found myself actually on my feet, half walking, half propelled[4] by medical equipment and members of my family. The orders were to walk the length and back of the long hospital corridor.

It was then that I first saw him. I saw him through a haze of drugs, pain and the dreamy unreality that this could be happening to me. He was standing in the doorway of a hospital room. In my twilight, unfocused state I saw him almost as a spirit shape rather than a full blown person. Yet the body language of this shape was somehow sending out sympathy and encouragement to me.

This became my daily routine for the next three weeks. As I gained a little more strength the man would be standing in the doorway, smiling and nodding as I would pass with one or more members of my family. On the fourth week I was allowed to solo up the corridor. As I passed his room, there was my faithful friend in the doorway. He was a slender dark

① fleecy['fliːsi] *adj.* 羊毛的，羊毛似的

② deli['deli] *n.* = delicatessen 熟食店

③ tavern['tævən] *n.* 酒菜馆

④ propel[prə'pel] *vt.* 推动，推进

complexioned man. I stopped a minute to chat. He introduced me to his wife and his son who was lying listlessly in a hospital bed. The next day as I made my scheduled walk, he came out and walked with me to my room. He explained that he and his wife had brought their teenage son to this hospital of hope from Iran. They were still hoping but things were not going well. He told me of how I had encouraged him on that first dreadful night's walking tour and how he was rooting① for me. For three more weeks we continued our conversations, each giving the other the gift of caring and friendship. He told me of how he enjoyed seeing my family as they rallied② around me and I was saddened by the loneliness of that small family so far from home.

Miraculously, there did come a day when the doctor told me I would be discharged③ the following morning. That night I told my friend. The next morning he came to my room. I had been up and dressed since dawn. My bright yellow dress gave me hope, and I almost looked human. We talked a bit. I told him I would pray for his son. He thanked me but shrugged his shoulders indicating the hopelessness. We knew we would never see each other again, in this world. This man in his sorrow was so happy for me. I felt his love. He took my hand and said, "You are my sister." I answered back and said, "You are my brother." He turned and left the room.

My family came to retrieve④ me. Doctors and nurses came to say their goodbyes and give orders. All business had been taken care of. After seven and a half weeks I was leaving the hospital room I had walked into

① root[ruːt] vi. 鼓气,捧场;欢呼;支持
② rally[ˈræli] vi. 团结;恢复
③ discharge[disˈtʃɑːdʒ] vt. 允许……离开;释放
④ retrieve[riˈtriːv] vt. 重新得到;取回;恢复

with so much trepidation. ①

As I turned to walk down the corridor to the elevator, my brother stood in the doorway, smiling, nodding and giving his blessing.

It was 14 years ago today on March 17th 1990 that I entered that operating room and much has happened to the world since my brother and I said our last farewell. Yet I think of him often and he is always in my heart as I feel I am in his. I remember his intense, dark brown eyes as we pledged ourselves as brother and sister. At that moment, I knew without a doubt that the Spirit of God hovered② over us smiling, nodding and blessing us with the knowledge that we are all one.

Many times I have pondered over the years why we humans meet our dearest friends or bond so deeply with another person when we are most vulnerable③. I think it is because when we face a life threatening illness, job loss, whatever the catastrophe may be, we are left completely without any pretension and our hearts and souls are open to those around us and we are able to accept the love and kindnesses of others, almost freely and thankfully as children accept love. This kind of love is blind to race, color and creed and leads to a pair of dark brown eyes seeking a pair of very blue eyes and pledging a love that will last through time.

情暖今生

时间早就过了午夜了，在雄伟威严的纽约医院，我裹在暖暖的羊毛睡袍里，静静地站在九楼病房的窗前凝视窗外。我看着眼前的第59街大桥，它像圣诞树般闪闪发光，美丽动人。在我心中，纽约一直有一个特别的位置，有百老汇的戏院，音乐，和形形色色、档次各异的餐馆。“这个城市本来就应该是这样的，”我想着，对即将到来的一天和它将带来的未知之数感到异常担心。但那天还是来了，就在那天，3月17日的早上9点，我被推进了手术室。11个小时45分钟后，我又被推进了疗养室，在被送回自己的病房后，仅

① trepidation[ˌtrepiˈdeiʃn] *n.* 发抖；惊慌

② hover[ˈhɔvə] *vi.* 盘旋，翱翔

③ vulnerable[ˈvʌlnərəbl] *adj.* 易受伤的，脆弱的

仅几个小时,我就已经能下地行走了,一半是自己在走,一半是被医疗器械和家人推着走。按医嘱,我要在医院的长廊里走一个来回。

就在那时,我第一次看到他。在药物和疼痛的作用下,透过朦胧的双眼,我看到了他,那景象就如同虚幻的梦境,我也不肯定自己究竟看到了什么。他当时正站在一间病房的门口。我当时正处于那种视力模糊的懵懂状态中,而他对我来说,就像个幽灵,而不是一个完整的人影。但我还是能感觉得到这个影像的身体语言中所流露出的对我的同情和鼓励。

在以后的三个星期里,在医院的长廊里行走成了我必做的功课。在我的力气稍微恢复之后,我在家人的陪同下走过他站立的门口,我会看到他站在那里向我微笑、点头。到了第四个星期,我可以自己在长廊上走了,每当我经过他的房间,我这位忠实的朋友都会站在门口。这是一个肤色稍黑、身体瘦小的男人。我停下来与他谈了一会儿。他把我介绍给他的妻子和儿子。他儿子没精打采地躺在病床上。第二天,我又按时地在走廊里走动,他从房间里走出来,陪我走回我的病房。他告诉我,他和他的妻子满怀希望地把他十几岁的儿子从伊朗带到这家医院。尽管现在他们还是抱有希望,但情况确实不容乐观。他告诉我,我手术后第一个难熬的晚上艰辛的行走使他受到了鼓舞,他也在暗暗为我加油。在接下来的三个多星期里,我们在一起交谈,互相关心,彼此关爱。他很高兴看到我的家人很关心和支持我,而我也为这个三口之家因远离家园而孤立无援而暗自伤感。

就像奇迹一般,终于有一天医生告诉我说,第二天我就可以出院了。那晚,我把这个消息告诉了我的朋友。第二天一早,他来到我的房间。那天,我早早地就起床了,并换好了衣服。我那鲜黄色的衣服给了我希望。我总算看起来又像个人了。我们俩谈了一会儿。我对他说,我会为他的儿子祈祷的。他在感谢我的同时,耸了耸肩,流露出失望之情。我们都知道在这个世界上,我们再也不会见面了。这个忧伤的人很为我感到高兴,我能感受到他对我的关爱。他握着我的手说:“你就是我的妹妹。”我回答道:“你就是我的哥哥。”说完,他转过身,走出了房间。

我的家人来接我了。医生和护士向我道别,嘱咐我出院后该怎么做。所有事情都安排得妥妥当当。在我怀着忐忑不安的心情走进医院的七个半星期后,我终于要离开我的病房了。

就在我沿着走廊向电梯走去时,我哥哥站在他的病房门口,冲我微笑点头,传递着他的祝福。

我进手术室的那天,也就是14年前的今天,1990年3月17日。自从我与我哥哥告别后，这个世界发生了很大的变化。但我还是经常会想起他，他一直都在我的心里，而我相信我也一直在他心中。我记得我们互称兄妹时，他那双真诚的深褐色的眼睛。在那一刻，我知道上帝正在天堂微笑地看着我们，向我们点头，为我们祝福。因为他知道，我们不分彼此。

在过去的岁月里，我不止一次在想，为什么人会在最脆弱的时候认识我们生命中最亲密的朋友，与另一个人结成最紧密的纽带也在这时结成。我认为，这是因为在我们面对危及生命的疾病、失业，或者其他灾难时，我们所有的伪装都会褪去，我们的心灵都会向周围的人敞开，接受来自他人的关爱和好意，差不多就像孩童那样，毫无芥蒂并心存感激承接爱。这种爱与种族、肤色、信仰无关，也正是这种爱，让那双深褐色的眼睛和那双深蓝色的眼睛相遇，并发誓永远彼此关爱。

24. Permission to Fail

Each of us fails from time to time. If we are wise, we accept these failures as a necessary part of the learning process. But all too often as parents and teachers we deny this same right to our children. We convey either by words or by actions that failure is something to be ashamed of, that nothing but top performance meets with our approval.

When I see a child subject to this kind of pressure, I think of Donnie.

Donnie was my youngest third-grader. He was a shy, nervous perfectionist①. His fear of failure kept him from classroom games that other children played with joyous② abandon. He seldom answered questions—he might be wrong. Written assignments, especially math, reduced him to nail-biting frustration③. He seldom finished his work because he repeatedly checked with me to be sure he hadn't made a mistake.

I tried my best to build his self-confidence. And I repeatedly asked God for direction. But nothing changed until midterm, when Mary Anne, a student teacher, was assigned to our classroom.

She was young and pretty, and she loved children. My pupils, Donnie included, adored her. But even enthusiastic④, loving Mary Anne was baffle⑤ by this little boy who feared he might make a mistake.

Then one morning we were working math problems at the chalkboard. Donnie had copied the problems with painstaking⑥ neatness and filled in answers for the first row. Pleased with his progress, I left the children with Mary Anne and went for art materials. When I returned, Donnie was in tears. He'd missed the third problem.

---

① perfectionist[pə'fekʃənist] *n.* 十全十美主义者,[哲]至善论者
② joyous['dʒɔiəs] *adj.* 快乐的,高兴的
③ frustration[frʌs'treiʃən] *n.* 挫败,挫折,受挫
④ enthusiastic[inˌθjuːzi'æstik] *adj.* 热心的,热情的
⑤ baffle['bæfl] *vt.* 阻碍,使挫折
⑥ painstaking['peinsteikiŋ] *adj.* 辛苦的,辛勤的,艰苦的

My student teacher looked at me in despair. Suddenly her face brightened. From the desk we shared, she got a canister① filled with pencils.

"Look, Donnie," she said, kneeling beside him and gently lifting the tear-stained face from his arms. "I've got something to show you." She removed the pencils, one at a time, and placed them on his desk.

"See these pencils, Donnie?" she continued. "They belong to Mrs. Lindstrom and me. See how the erasers are worn? That's because we make mistakes too. Lots of them. But we erase the mistakes and try again. That's what you must learn to do, too."

She kissed him and stood up. "Here," she said, "I'll leave one of these pencils on your desk so you'll remember that everybody makes mistakes, even teachers." Donnie looked up with love in his eyes and just a glimmer of a smile—the first I'd see on his face that year.

The pencil became Donnie's prized possession. That, together with Mary Anne's frequent encouragement and unfailing praise for even Donnie's small successes, gradually persuaded him that it's all right to make mistakes—as long as you erase them and try again.

允许失败

我们每个人都会经历一次又一次的失败。如果足够明智,我们就会把这些失败看做学习过程中的必修课。然而,作为父母和老师的我们,对孩子们往往否定这一权利。我们要么说出来,要么用行动表示出来:失败是可耻的,我们只赞同欣赏优异的表现。

每每看到某个孩子怀有这样的压力,我会想到多尼。

多尼是我教的三年级中最小的一个学生。他是一位容易害羞、紧张的完美主义者。他害怕失败,所以就不能尽情地和其他孩子一起玩耍。他很少回答问题——他可能会犯错。书面作业,尤其是数学,会让他沮丧得束手无策。他很少完成作业,因为他不断地向我核对,确保自己不会犯错。

我想尽一切方法给他树立自信心。我也经常向上帝寻求指引。可是情

① canister[ˈkænistə]n.(放咖啡、茶叶、烟等的)小罐,筒

况没有一点点改变，直到下半学期到来，一位实习教师，玛丽·安，分配到我们班，情况才有所改观。

年轻漂亮的玛丽特别喜欢孩子。我的学生们，包括多尼，都非常喜欢她。然而，尽管满怀激情，富有爱心的玛丽·安被这位害怕犯错的小男生难住了。

后来，一天上午，我们在黑板上做着数学题目。多尼费力地把黑板上的题目工工整整地抄写下来，然后对第一行的题目填写答案。对他的进步感到满意，我就把孩子们交给了玛丽·安，去拿美术资料。我回来的时候，看到多尼正在流泪。原来，他错过了第三道题目。

我的实习老师用绝望的目光看着我，突然她的面容一亮。从我们共用的桌子里面，她拿出来了盛满铅笔的小筒。

“瞧，多尼，”她说，双膝蹲在他的旁边，温柔地把他沾满泪水的脸蛋从他的手臂中抬起。“我让你看些东西。”她把那些铅笔从笔筒中依次拿出来，放在他的课桌上。

“多尼，看这些铅笔?”她继续说。“这些是我和林达斯多姆夫人的铅笔。你看看这上面的橡皮有多旧？这是因为我们也犯错。犯了很多错。可是我们把这些错擦去然后再试。这也是你必须学会的。”

她吻了一下多尼，然后站了起来。“那么，”她说，“我会把其中一支铅笔放在你的桌子上，你会记得我们每个人都会犯错，即使是老师也不例外。”多尼抬起头来，眼睛里充满暖意同时脸上还带有一丝笑意——那年我第一次看到他有那样的表情。

那支铅笔成了多尼珍贵的财富。此后，即使多尼有了一点点的进步，玛丽·安也会不断地鼓励、表扬多尼，渐渐地让他意识到犯错是多么正常——只要把它们擦掉再试就好了。

25. If I Were a Boy Again

If I were a boy again, I would practice perseverance① more often, and never give up a thing because it was hard or inconvenient. If we want light, we must conquer darkness. Perseverance can sometimes equal genius in its results. "There are only two creatures," says a proverb, "who can surmount the pyramids—the eagle and the snail."

If I were a boy again, I would school myself into a habit of attention; I would let nothing come between me and the subject in hand. I would remember that a good skater never tries to skate in two directions at once.

The habit of attention becomes part of our life, if we begin early enough. I often hear grown-up people say "I could not fix my attention on the sermon or book, although I wished to do so", and the reason is, the habit was not formed in youth.

If I were to live my life over again, I would pay more attention to the cultivation of the memory. I would strengthen that faculty by every possible means, and on every possible occasion. It takes a little hard work at first to remember things accurately; but memory soon helps itself, and gives very little trouble. It only needs early cultivation to become a power.

If I were a boy again, I would cultivate courage. "Nothing is so mild and gentle as courage, nothing so cruel and pitiless as cowardice②," says a wise author.

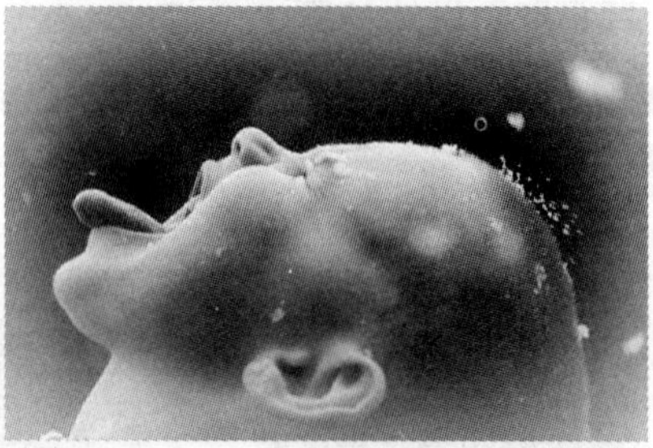

We too often borrow trouble, and anticipate that may never appear. "The fear of ill exceeds the ill we fear." Dangers will arise in any

---

① perseverance[ˌpəsiˈviərəns] *n.* 毅力

② cowardice[ˈkauədis] *n.* 懦弱,胆怯

career, but presence of mind will often conquer the worst of them. Be prepared for any fate, and there is no harm to be feared.

If I were a boy again, I would look on the cheerful side. Life is very much like a mirror: if you smile upon it, it smiles back upon you; but if you frown and look doubtful on it, you will get a similar look in return.

Inner sunshine warms not only the heart of the owner, but of all that come in contact with it. "Who shuts love out, in turn shall be shut out from love."

If I were a boy again, I would school myself to say no more often. I might write pages on the importance of learning very early in life to gain that point where a young boy can stand erect, and decline doing an unworthy act because it is unworthy.

If I were a boy again, I would demand of myself more courtesy towards my companions and friends, and indeed towards strangers as well. The smallest courtesies along the rough roads of life are like the little birds that sing to us all winter long, and make that season of ice and snow more endurable.

Finally, instead of trying hard to be happy, as if that were the sole purpose of life, I would, if I were a boy again, I would still try harder to make others happy.

假如我又回到了童年

假如我又回到了童年,我做事要更有毅力,决不因为事情艰难或者麻烦而撒手不干。我们要光明,就得征服黑暗。毅力在效果上有时能同天才相比。俗话说:"能登上金字塔的生物,只有两种——鹰和蜗牛。"

假如我又回到了童年,我就要养成专心致志的习惯;有事在手,就决不让任何东西让我分心。我要牢记:优秀的滑冰手从不试图同时滑向两个不同的方向。

如果及早养成这种专心致志的习惯,它将成为我们生命的一部分。我常听成年人说:"虽然我希望能集中注意听牧师讲道或读书,但往往做不到。"而原因就是年轻时没有养成这种习惯。

假如我现在能重新开始我的生命,我就要更注意记忆力的培养。我要采取一切可能的办法，并且在一切可能的场合，增强记忆力。要正确无误地记住一些东西，在开始阶段的确要作出一番小小的努力；但要不了多久，记忆力本身就会起作用，使记忆成为轻而易举的事，只需及早培养，记忆自会成为一种才能。

假如我又回到了童年，我就要培养勇气。一位明智的作家曾说过："世上没有东西比勇气更温文尔雅，也没有东西比懦弱更残酷无情。"

我们常常过多地自寻烦恼，杞人忧天。"怕祸害比祸害本身更可怕。"凡事都有危险，但镇定沉着往往能克服最严重的危险。对一切祸福做好准备，那么就没有什么灾难可以害怕的了。

假如我又回到了童年，我就要事事乐观。生活犹如一面镜子：你朝它笑，它也朝你笑；如果你双眉紧锁，向它投以怀疑的目光，它也将还以你同样的目光。

内心的欢乐不仅温暖了欢乐者自己的心，也温暖了所有与之接触者的心。"谁拒爱于门外，也必将被爱拒诸门外。"

假如我又回到了童年，我就要养成经常说"不"字的习惯。一个少年要能挺得起腰，拒绝做不应该做的事，就因为这事不值得做。我可以写上好几页谈谈早年培养这一点的重要性。

假如我又回到了童年，我就要要求自己对伙伴和朋友更加礼貌，而且对陌生人也应如此。在坎坷的生活道路上，最细小的礼貌犹如在漫长的冬天为我们歌唱的小鸟，那歌声使冰天雪地的寒冬变得较易忍受。

最后，假如我又回到了童年，我不会力图为自己谋幸福，好像这就是人生唯一的目的；与之相反，我要更努力为他人谋幸福。

26. The Pleasure of Reading

All the wisdom of the ages, all the stories that delighted mankind for centuries, are easily and cheaply available① to all of us within the covers of books, but we must know how to avail ourselves of this treasure and how to get the most value from it. The unfortunate people in the world are those who have never discovered how satisfying it is to read good books.

I am most interested in people, in them and finding out about them. Some of the remarkable② people I've met exited in writer's imagination, then on the pages of his book, and then again, in my imagination. I have found in books new friend, new society and new words.

If I am interested in people, others are interested not so much in who as in how. Who in the books includes everybody from science fiction superman two hundred years in the future all the way back to the first figure in history. Who covers from the ingenious③ explanations of Sherlock Holmes to the discoveries of science and the ways of teaching manners to children?

Reading is pleasure of the mind which means that it is a little like a sport: your eagerness and knowledge and quickness make you a good reader. Reading is fun, not because the writer telling you something, but because it makes your mind work. Your own imagination works along with the author's or even goes beyond his. Your experience, compared with his, brings you to the same or different conclusion and

① available[ə'veiləbl] *adj.* 可用到的，可利用的
② remarkable[ri'mɑːkəbl] *adj.* 不平常的，非凡的，值得注意的，显著的
③ ingenious[in'dʒiːnjəs] *adj.* 机灵的，有独创性的

your ideas develop as you understand his.

Every book stands by itself, like a one-family house, but books in library like a house in a city. Although they are separated, together they add up to something, they are connected with others and with other cities. The same or the related ones, turns up in different places, the humans that repeated in life repeated themselves in literature, but different solution according to the different writings and different times. Books influence each others; they link the past, the present and the futures, and have their own generations, like family. Whenever you start reading you connect yourself with one of the families of ideas, and in the long run, you not only find out about the world and the people in it; you find out about yourself too.

Reading can only be fun, if you expect it to be. If you concentrate on books somebody tell you you "ought" to read, you probably won't have fun. If you put down a book you don't like and try another till you find one means something to you, and then relax with it, you may almost certainly have a good time—and if you become, as a result of reading, better, wiser, kinder, gentle, you won't have suffered during the process.

读书的乐趣

岁月沉淀的智慧，千年不衰的故事，只要打开扉页，我们便可轻易获得。但是，如何拥有这些瑰宝，如何掌握其中精华，却是我们最应该了解的知识。那些无法从佳作经典中获得愉悦和满足的人，才是这个世界中最为不幸的人。

我对书中的人物最感兴趣，追寻着他们的足迹，期待着与其聚首。至今最让我难忘的人物产生于作家的想象之中，其次驻留在书页之上，再次则徘徊在我的思绪当中。唯在品味佳作的过程中，我方能觅得新朋友，窥见新境界，收获新词汇。

设若我对书中的人物感兴趣，其他人则可能更在意这些人是谁而不是他们做了什么。"这些人是谁"将科幻小说中两百个世纪之后的超人和历史记载里的第一人统统纳入;“他们做了什么”则涵盖了福尔摩斯神探的机敏解释、科学研究中的众多发现以及儿童教育的方法,等等。

读书,其实与游戏类似,是一种心灵的愉悦:热情、知识以及速度有助于你成为一个好的读者。读书令人趣味盎然,这并非源自于作者故事的诉说,而是因为对读者思维的促动,你的想象与作者的叙述相伴而飞,甚而超越作者;你的经历与作者的故事相映成趣,给予或同或异的体验——当你在理解作者想法的过程中,你的思维同时获得升华。

一本书本身就像一间房子,而图书馆中的书则像一个城市中的建筑。尽管它们相互独立,但却彼此相连,甚至与其他城市中的也有联系,从而组成了一个有机的整体。相同或相关的思想在不同的地方出现。生活中反复出现的问题同样在文学作品中也反复出现,只是在不同时期的不同作品中给出了不同的解释。书籍之间也相互影响;它们联结着过去、现在和未来,像家族一样,它们也有自己的后代。无论何时你开始阅读,你便将自己与一个书籍家族的思想联系在一起,最后,你不仅在书中认识了世界,认识了书中的人物,也认识了你自己。

读一本自己想读的书是件愉快的事。倘若人云亦云,去读那些别人推荐的书,你可能体验不到快乐。放下你不喜欢的书,试着去读另一本书,直到你发现它很有意思,然后去品味它,这样你一定会感到读书是一件很愉快的事。读书会让你变得更加完善,更有智慧,更和善,更文雅,这样你再也不会感到读书是件痛苦的事。

27. Mother's Hands

Night after night, she came to tuck me in, even long after my childhood years. Following her longstanding custom, she'd lean down and push my long hair out of the way, then kiss my forehead.

I don't remember when it first started annoying me—her hands pushing my hair that way. But it did annoy me, for they felt work-worn and rough against my young skin. Finally, one night, I shouted out at her, "Don't do that anymore—your hands are too rough!" She didn't say anything in reply. But never again did my mother close out my day with that familiar expression of her love.

Time after time, with the passing years, my thoughts returned to that night. By then I missed my mother's hands, missed her goodnight kiss on my forehead. Sometimes the incident seemed very close, sometimes far away. But always it lurked, in the back of my mind.

Well, the years have passed, and I'm not a little girl anymore. Mom is in her mid-seventies, and those hands I once thought to be so rough are still doing things for me and my family. She's been our doctor, reaching into a medicine cabinet for the remedy to calm a young girl's stomach or soothe the boy's scraped knee. She cooks the best fried chicken in the world... gets stains out of blue jeans like I never could...

Now, my own children are grown and gone. Mom no longer has Dad, and on special occasions, I find myself drawn next door to spend the night with her. So it was late on Thanksgiving Eve, as I slept in the bedroom of my youth, a familiar hand hesitantly run across my face to brush the hair from my forehead. Then a kiss, ever so gently, touched my brow.

In my memory, for the thousandth time, I recalled the night my young voice complained, "Don't do that anymore—your hands are too rough!" Catching Mom's hand in hand, I blurted out how sorry I was for that night. I thought she'd remember, as I did. But Mom didn't know what I was talking about. She had forgotten—and forgiven—long ago.

That night,I fell asleep with a new appreciation for my gentle mother and her caring hands. And the guilt that I had carried around for so long was nowhere to be found.

母亲的手

夜复一夜,她总是来帮我把被子掖好,即使我早已不是小孩子了。掖好被子后,她会弯下身来,拨开我的长发,在我的额头上吻一下。这是母亲长久以来的习惯。

不记得从何时起,我开始讨厌她用手拨开我的头发。但我的确讨厌她长期操劳、粗糙的手触摸我细嫩的皮肤。终于,一天晚上,我冲她嚷道:“别再这样了——你的手太粗糙了!”母亲什么也没说。但从此之后,她再也没有在一天结束的时候用那种熟悉的方式表达她的爱。

时光流逝,许多年之后,我的思绪又回到了那个晚上。那时我想念母亲的手,想念她晚上留在我额头上的亲吻。有时这幕情景似乎很近,有时又似乎很遥远。可它总是潜伏着,时常浮现在我的意识中。

一年年过去,我也不再是一个小女孩,母亲也有70多岁了。那双我认为很粗糙的手依然为我和我的家庭操劳着。她是我家的医生,去药橱给我胃疼的女儿找胃药或为我儿子擦伤的膝盖敷药。她能做出世界上最美味的炸鸡……能洗掉牛仔裤上那些我永远都弄不干净的污点……

现在,我的孩子都已经长大,离开了家,爸爸也去世了。在一些特别的日子里,我经常情不自禁地走到隔壁母亲的房间和她一起度过。于是,一次感恩节前夕的深夜,我睡在年轻时住的卧室里,一只熟悉的手有些犹豫地掠过我的脸,拨开我额头的头发,随后是一个吻,轻轻地印在我的眉毛上。

在我的记忆中,无数次回想起年轻时那晚我抱怨的声音:“别再这样了——你的手太粗糙了!”抓住母亲的手,我脱口而出地表示我多么后悔那晚所说的话。我以为她会像我一样记得这件事情。但妈妈不知道我在说些什么,她已经在很久以前就忘了这事,并早就原谅了我。

那晚,我带着对温柔的母亲和她体贴的双手的全新认识进入了梦乡。而我许久以来的负罪感也消失得无影无踪。

28. The Colors of the Rainbow

Once upon a time the colors of the world started to quarrel: all claimed that they were the best, the most important, the most useful, the favorite.

GREEN said: "Clearly I am the most important. I am the sign of life and of hope. I was chosen for grass, trees, leaves—without me, all animals would die. Look over the countryside and you will see that I am in the majority."

BLUE interrupted①: "You only think about the earth, but consider the sky and the sea. It is the water that is the basis of life and, drawn up by the clouds, forms the deep sea. The sky gives space and peace and serenity②. Without my peace, you would all be nothing."

YELLOW chuckled: "You are all so serious. I bring laughter, gaiety③, and warmth into the world. The sun is yellow, the moon is yellow, the stars are yellow. Every time you look at a sunflower, the whole world starts to smile. Without me there would be no fun."

ORANGE started next to blow her trumpet: "I am the color of health and strength. I may be scarce, but I am precious for I serve the needs of human life. I carry the most important vitamins. Think of carrots, pumpkins, oranges, mangoes, and papaws. I don't hang around all the time, but when I fill the sky at sunrise or sunset, my beauty is so striking that no one gives another thought to any of you."

RED could stand it no longer. He shouted out: "I am the ruler of all of you—I am blood—life's blood! I am the color of danger and of bravery. I am willing to fight for a cause. I bring fire into the blood. Without me, the earth would

---

① interrupt[ˌintəˈrʌpt] *v.* 打断

② serenity[siˈreniti] *n.* 平静

③ gaiety[ˈgeiəti] *n.* 快乐、高兴

be empty as the moon. I am the color of passion and of love, the red rose, the poinsettia① and the poppy."

PURPLE rose up to his full height. He was very tall and spoke with great pomp: "I am the color of royalty② and power. Kings, chiefs, and bishops have always chosen me for I am the sign of authority and wisdom. People do not question me—they listen and obey."

Finally, INDIGO spoke, much more quietly than all the others, but with just as much determination③: "Think of me. I am the color of silence. You hardly notice me, but without me you all become superficial④. I represent thought and reflection, twilight⑤ and deep water. You need me for balance and contrast, for prayer and inner peace."

And so the colors went on boasting, each convinced of his or her own superiority⑥. Their quarreling became louder and louder. Suddenly there was a startling flash of bright lightening—thunder rolled and boomed. Rain started to pour down relentlessly⑦. The colors crouched⑧ down in fear, drawing close to one another for comfort.

In the midst of the clamor, rain began to speak: "You foolish colors, fighting amongst yourselves, each trying to dominate the rest. Don't you know that you were each made for a special purpose, unique and different? Join hands with one another and come to me."

Doing as they were told, the colors united and joined hands. The rain continued: "From now on, when it rains, each of you will stretch across the sky in a great bow of color as a reminder that you can all live in peace. The RAINBOW is a sign of hope for tomorrow."

① poinsettia[pɔinˈsetiə] *n.* 一品红,猩猩木
② royalty[ˈrɔiəlti] *n.* 皇室,王权
③ determination[diˌtəːmiˈneiʃən] *n.* 决心,果断
④ superficial[ˌsjuːpəˈfiʃəl] *adj.* 表面的,肤浅的,浅薄的
⑤ twilight[ˈtwailait] *n.* 黎明,微光
⑥ superiority[sju(ː)ˌpiəriˈɔriti] *n.* 优越,高傲
⑦ relentlessly[riˈlentlisli] *adv.* 无情地,残酷地
⑧ crouch[ˈkrautʃ] *v.* 蜷缩,蹲伏

And so, whenever a good rain washes the world, and a rainbow appears in the sky, let us remember to appreciate① one another.

彩虹的颜色

很久很久以前,世界上的颜色们发生了一次争吵:所有的颜色都声称自己是最好、最重要、最有用、最受人喜爱的颜色。

绿色说:“显然,我是最重要的。我是生命和希望的标记。我是青草、树木、树叶的颜色——没有我,所有的动物就会死去。眺望一下田野,你们就会发现大部分都充斥着绿色。”

蓝色打断他说:“你只想到了地球,再看看天空和海洋。水是生命的源泉,被云彩吸收后形成了深海。天空给予了空间和平和宁静。没有我的和平,你们将烟消云散。”

黄色咯咯笑了起来:“你们这么严肃干吗。我为世界带来了笑声、欢乐和温暖。太阳是黄色的,月亮是黄色的,星星也是黄色的。每次,你们看到向日葵时,整个世界开始笑了。没有我世界将毫无生气。”

接着橙色开始大肆渲染起来:“我是健康和力量的颜色。我可能很稀少,却很珍贵,因为我效劳于人类生命的基本需要。我携带的维生素最多。想想胡萝卜、南瓜、橙子、芒果还有木瓜。我并不是一直出现,而当日出或日落时分我充斥着天空时,我的美丽是如此的惊人,没有人会想起你们中任何一个。”

红色再也受不了了。他叫嚷着:“我是你们的统治者——我是血——生命的血!我是危险和勇敢的颜色。我愿意为了一项事业而奋斗。我为血液注入了活力。没有我,地球就会像月球那样一片荒芜,没有生机。我是激情和爱的颜色,红玫瑰、一品红和罂粟都是红色。”

紫色站得笔直。他高高的个子,用傲慢的口吻说:“我是高贵和权力的颜色。国王、酋长、还有教皇总是选择我因为我是权力和智慧的象征。人们不会对我质疑——只是听从和顺从我。”

① appreciate[ə'priːʃieit] *v.* 赏识,鉴赏,感激

最后,青色说话了,他比其他任何颜色都要平静得多,但口气却格外坚定:“想想我,我是沉默的颜色。你们几乎注意不到我,可是没有我你们就会变得肤浅。我代表着思索和沉思,晨曦和深水。为了保持平衡和对比,你们需要我;为了祈祷和内心的安宁,你们需要我。”

就这样,这些颜色们继续吹嘘着自己的价值,每种颜色都想让别人信服他或她的优越感。他们的吵声越来越大。突然,一道闪电划过天际——接着雷声隆隆。漂泊大雨无情地倾泻而下。这些颜色们惊恐地蹲了下来,相互依偎寻求安慰。

喧嚣中,雨开始说话了:“你们这些愚蠢的颜色们,竟然相互攻击,谁都想试图统治其他人。你们难道不知道你们每个人都有自己的独特之处,并且各自有特殊的用途吗?快点携起手到我这里来吧。”

按照雨的吩咐,这些颜色们牵起手来聚在一起。雨继续说:“从现在开始,为了证明你们能够和平相处,每次下雨,你们每人都要以彩色的巨弓方式在空中伸展自己。雨中的弓(彩虹)象征着明天充满希望。”

于是,只要有场酣畅淋漓的大雨冲刷世界,空中就会出现一道彩虹,让我们学会欣赏彼此吧。

29. It's Never Too Late

Several years ago, while attending a communications course, I experienced a most unusual process. The instructor asked us to list anything in our past that we felt ashamed of, guilty about, regretted, or incomplete about. The next week he invited participants to read their lists aloud. This seemed like a very private① process, but there's always some brave soul in the crowd who will volunteer. As people read their lists, mine grew longer. After three weeks, I had 101 items on my list. The instructor then suggested that we find ways to make amends, apologize to people, or take some action to right any wrongdoing. I was seriously wondering how this could ever improve my communications, having visions of alienating② just about everyone from my life.

The next week, the man next to me raised his hand and volunteered this story:

"While making my list, I remembered an incident from high school. I grew up in a small town in Iowa. There was a sheriff③ in town that none of us kids liked. One night, my two buddies and I decided to play a trick on Sheriff Brown. After drinking a few beers, we found a can of red paint, climbed the tall water tank in the middle of town, and wrote, on the tank, in bright red letters: Sheriff Brown is an s. o. b. ④ The next day, the town arose to see our glorious⑤ sign. Within two hours, Sheriff Brown

① private['praivit] *adj.* 私人的,私有的,私营的,秘密的

② alienating['eiljəneitiŋ] *v.* 疏远

③ sheriff['ʃerif] *n.* 郡长

④ s. o. b abbr. Son of a Bitch 畜生,狗娘养的

⑤ glorious['glɔːriəs] *adj.* 光荣的,显赫的

had my two pals and me in his office. My friends confessed① and I lied, denying the truth. No one ever found out.

"Nearly 20 years later, Sheriff Brown's name appears on my list. I didn't even know if he was still alive. Last weekend, I dialed information in my hometown back in Iowa. Sure enough, there was a Roger Brown still listed. I dialed his number. After a few rings, I heard: 'Hello?' I said: 'Sheriff Brown?' Pause. 'Yup.' 'Well, this is Jimmy Calkins. And I want you to know that I did it.' Pause. 'I knew it!' he yelled back. We had a good laugh and a lively discussion. His closing words were: 'Jimmy, I always felt badly for you because your buddies got it off their chest, and I knew you were carrying it around all these years. I want to thank you for calling me… for your sake.'"

Jimmy inspired me to clear up all 101 items on my list. It took me almost two years, but became the springboard and true inspiration② for my career as a conflict mediator③. No matter how difficult the conflict, crisis or situation, I always remember that it's never too late to clear up the past and begin resolution④.

决不太晚

几年前，我参加了一个有关人际交流课程，其间我有过这样一次非同寻常的经历。老师要求我们将过去那些感到羞耻的、愧疚的、遗憾的或悔恨的事情列举出来。一周后他请大家大声宣读自己所列清单。这看起来有点涉及隐私，却总有人自告奋勇。听了别人的陈述之后我的清单愈发长了起来。3 周后，我的清单上竟达 101 条之多。后来，老师建议我们想法弥补缺憾，向

① confess[kən'fes] *v.* 承认，坦白，忏悔
② inspiration[ˌinspə'reiʃən] *n.* 灵感
③ mediator['miːdieitə] *n.* 调停者，仲裁人
④ resolution[ˌrezə'luːʃən] *n.* 坚定，决心，决定，决议

别人真诚道歉,或采取行动来纠正自己的过失。我对此举能否增进我的人际关系深表疑惑,相反却认为这只能使彼此更加疏远。

到了下周,坐在我身旁的那位男士举手自愿讲述了这个故事:

“我在列举清单时,想起高中时发生的一件事情,我在衣阿华州的一个小镇长大。镇上有个我们孩子们都讨厌的郡长。有天晚上,我和两个伙伴决定要捉弄这个叫布朗的郡长。喝了几瓶啤酒之后,我们找到一罐红颜料,我们爬到镇子中央的高高水塔之上,在上面用鲜红的颜料写道:布朗是个狗娘养的。第二天,镇上的人们起来后都看到了我们的‘大作’。两小时后,布朗把我们3个人弄到他的办公室。我的伙计们承认了错误而我却撒谎抵赖,蒙混过关。从此没有人知道真相。

“这件事都快过去20年了。今天布朗郡长的名字出现在我的清单上。我甚至不知道他是否还在人世。上个周末,我给衣阿华州的家乡打电话查问,果然有个叫罗杰·布朗的先生。我于是给他打电话。铃声响了几下后,我听到:‘喂,你好。’我问:‘是布朗郡长吗?’那边沉默了一下,‘是的。’‘那好,我是吉米·考金斯。我想告诉你那事我也有份。’又是沉默。‘我早就知道!’他大声回应。我们于是大笑,相谈得很愉快。他最后说:‘吉米,我一直为你感到不安,因为你的伙伴们都已摘掉了心病,而你这么多年却一直挂在心上。我想应该感谢你打来电话……这是为你着想。’”

吉米鼓励我化解我清单上的101条。这费了我近2年的时间,但这却成了我以后从事矛盾调解工作的起点和动力。不论冲突、纠纷或处境多么严重,我一直记着摒弃前嫌,化解宿怨,亡羊补牢,为时不晚。

30. Run Through the Rain

She had been shopping with her Mom in Wal-Mart. She must have been 6 years old, this beautiful brown haired, freckle-faced image of innocence①. It was pouring outside. The kind of rain that gushes over the top of rain gutters, so much in a hurry to hit the Earth it has no time to flow down the spout.

We all stood there under the awning and just inside the door of the Wal-Mart. We waited, some patiently, others irritated because nature messed up their hurried day. I am always mesmerized② by rainfall. I get lost in the sound and sight of the heavens washing away③ the dirt and dust of the world. Memories of running, splashing so carefree as a child come pouring in as a welcome reprieve④ from the worries of my day.

Her voice was so sweet as it broke the hypnotic⑤ trance we were all caught in. "Mom, let's run through the rain," she said.

"What?" Mom asked.

"Let's run through the rain!" She repeated.

"No, honey. We'll wait until it slows down a bit," Mom replied.

This young child waited about another minute and repeated: "Mom, let's run through the rain."

"We'll get soaked if we do," Mom said.

"No, we won't, Mom. That's not what you said this morning," the young girl said as she tugged at her Mom's arm.

"This morning? When did I say we could run through the rain and not get wet?"

① innocence[ˈinəsns] n. 单纯,天真无邪,清白

② mesmerize[ˈmezməraiz] v. 施催眠术

③ washing away 冲刷

④ reprieve[riˈpriːv] n. 暂缓,缓刑

⑤ hypnotic[hipˈnɔtik] adj. 催眠的,易被催眠的

"Don't you remember? When you were talking to Daddy about his cancer, you said, 'If God can get us through this, he can get us through anything!'"

The entire crowd stopped dead silent. I swear you couldn't hear anything but the rain. We all stood silently. No one came or left in the next few minutes. Mom paused and thought for a moment about what she would say.

Now some would laugh it off① and scold her for being silly. Some might even ignore what was said. But this was a moment of affirmation② in a young child's life. Time when innocent trust can be nurtured so that it will bloom into faith. "Honey, you are absolutely right. Let's run through the rain. If get wet, well maybe we just needed washing," Mom said. Then off they ran.

We all stood watching, smiling and laughing as they darted past the cars. They held their shopping bags over their heads just in case. They got soaked. But they were followed by a few who screamed and laughed like children all the way to their cars. And yes, I did. I ran. I got wet. I needed washing. Circumstances or people can take away your material possessions, they can take away your money, and they can take away your health. But no one can ever take away your precious memories. So, don't forget to make time and take the opportunities to make memories every day!

To everything there is a season and a time to every purpose under heaven. I hope you still take the time to run through the rain.

雨中狂奔

她和妈妈刚在沃尔玛购物。这个天真的女孩应该6岁大了，头发是美

① laugh off 用笑摆脱

② affirmation[əfəːˈmeiʃən] *n.* 断言，主张

丽的棕色,脸上有雀斑。外面下着倾盆大雨。雨水溢满了檐槽,来不及排走,就迫不及待地涌向了大地。

我们都站在沃尔玛的遮篷下和门里面。大家在等待,有的人很耐心,也有人烦躁,因为老天在给他们本已忙碌的一天添乱。雨天总引起我的遐思。我出神地听着、看着老天洗刷冲走这世界的污垢和尘埃,孩时无忧无虑地在雨中奔跑玩水的记忆汹涌而至,暂时缓解了我这一天的焦虑。

女孩甜美的声音打破了这令人昏昏欲睡的气氛,"妈妈,我们在雨里跑吧,"她说。

"什么?"母亲问。

"我们在雨里跑吧!"她重复道。

"不,亲爱的,我们等雨小一点再走,"母亲回答说。

过了一会小女孩又说:"妈妈,我们在雨里跑吧。"

"这样的话我们会湿透的,"母亲说。

"不会的,妈妈。你今天早上不是这样说的。"小女孩一边说,一边拉着母亲的胳膊。

"今天早上?我什么时候说过我们淋雨不会湿啊?"

"你不记得了吗?你和爸爸谈他的癌症时,你不是说'如果上帝让我们闯过这一关,那我们就没有什么过不去了。'"

人群一片寂静。我发誓,除了雨声,你什么都听不到。我们都静静地站着。接下来的几分钟没有一个人走动。母亲停了一下,在想着应该说些什么。

有人也许会对此一笑了之,或者责备这孩子的不懂事,有人甚至不把她的话放在心上。但这却是一个小孩子一生中需要被肯定的时候。若受到鼓舞,此时孩子单纯的信任就会发展成为坚定的信念。"亲爱的,你说的对,我们跑过去吧。如果淋湿了,那也许是因为我们的确需要冲洗一下了,"母亲说。然后她们就冲出去了。

我们都站在那里,笑着看她们飞快地跑过那些停着的汽车。她们把购物袋高举过头想挡挡雨,但还是湿透了。好几个人像孩子般尖叫着,大笑着,也跟着冲了出去，奔向自己的车子。当然，我也这样做了，跑了出去，淋湿了。我也需要接受洗礼。环境或其他人可以夺去你的物质财富，抢走你的金钱，带走你的健康，但没有人可以带走你珍贵的回忆。因此，记得要抓紧时间，抓住机会每天都给自己留下一些回忆吧！

世间万物皆有自己的季节，做任何事情也有一个恰当的时机。希望你有机会在雨中狂奔一回。

31. Something Worth Thinking about

How many times have you heard the expression that most people spend more time planning their vacation than they do planning their lives? I would expand that expression by adding that most people spend more time "thinking" about their vacation than they do thinking about what's important in their life.

While rest and relaxation① are a must in living a balanced life, it's not what we were created to do. After all, the Master Creator took his R&R (Rest and Recreation) on the seventh day, only after six days of "definitely directed thought".

Wallace D. Wattles wrote: "There is no labor from which most people shrink as they do from that of sustained② and consecutive③ thought; it is the hardest work in the world." And yet it is the first and primary labor of achievement.

My friend Mike Litman wrote an outstanding article this week. It's called "The Millionaire Composite" and it analyzes one of the big differences between super-successful people and everyone else. He writes "I recently visited with a Real Estate Multi Millionaire Mogul. What did I see next to his desk? His vision statement, along with a list of what he values in life—hand written.

"A few months back, I interviewed an individual who has sold over a billion dollars worth of products on television. He told me that he reads his life and business vision and goals daily , and that he TAKES TIME to

① relaxation[ˌriːlæk'seiʃən] *n.* 松弛,放宽,缓和
② sustained[səs'teind] *adj.* 持续不变的,相同的
③ consecutive[kən'sekjutiv] *adj.* 连续的,连贯的

visualize① exactly what he wants to create—EACH NIGHT before falling asleep."

What is your life's purpose or your personal mission statement? Is it written down? Do you review it and think about it often? Is your life organized around your purpose and a set of goals that support that purpose?

Without purpose and goals—definitely directed thought—you are like the proverbial②"ship without a rudder". There is power in your purpose and in your goals. It is the power that takes you over obstacles, the fuel that propels③ you toward the life you envision④.

One of my favorite passages of James Allen is one he wrote in "The Mastery of Destiny":

"All successful people are people of purpose. They hold fast to an idea, a project, a plan, and will not let it go; they cherish⑤ it, brood upon it, tend and develop it; and when assailed⑥ by difficulties, they refuse to be beguiled⑦ into surrender; indeed, the intensity of the purpose increases with the growing magnitude⑧ of the obstacles encountered." And that's worth thinking about.

值得思考的事情

多少次你曾听到过这样的论点：大多数人在规划假期上花的时间比他们在规划自己生活上花的时间要多？我为这一观点做了一点延伸：大多数的人在"考虑"假期上花的时间比他们在考虑人生中重要的事情上花的时间要多。

① visualize[ˈvizjuəlaiz] *v.* 形象，形象化，想象
② proverbial[prəˈvəːbiəl] *adj.* 谚语的，谚语式的，众所周知的，公认的
③ propel[prəˈpel] *v.* 推进，驱使
④ envision[inˈviʒən] *v.* 想象，预想
⑤ cherish[ˈtʃeriʃ] *v.* 珍爱，怀抱（希望等）
⑥ assail[əˈseil] *v.* 攻击，质问
⑦ beguile[biˈgail] *v.* 诱骗，诱惑
⑧ magnitude[ˈmægnitjuːd] *n.* 大小，数量，巨大

虽然休息和放松是平衡生活的必要元素，但是我们并不是为了它们而活着。毕竟，伟大的造物主在前6天的“明确的方向性思考”后，第七天才休息和放松。

华莱士·D·华佗士写道：“没有任何一种体力劳动能够使大多数人望而却步，但连续不断的持久思考却能做到这一点；它是这世界上最困难的工作。”它却也是取得成功首先要做的重要的劳动。

我的朋友迈克·里特曼本周写了一篇杰出的文章，名叫《百万富翁的构造》，其中分析了超级成功者与其他人的一个重要区别。他写道：“我最近拜访了一位房地产界腰缠数百万的大亨。你们猜我看见他桌旁放了些什么？他对自己梦想的描述和一张列有生活中值得珍惜之物的清单——都是手写的。

“几个月前，我采访了另一位获得巨大成功的商人，他通过电视节目卖出的产品总价值超过10亿美元。他告诉我：每天他都思考生活和事业中自己的梦想与目标，他花时间将他想要实现的理想在脑海中形象化——每晚睡觉前都这样做。”

你的人生目标和个人使命是什么？你把它们都写下来了吗？你经常回顾并思考它们吗？你的生活是围绕着理想和一系列相关的目标而安排的吗？

如果没有理想和目标——明确的方向性思考——你就会像俗语说的“一条没有舵的船”。理想和目标中蕴含着力量。它是使你越过障碍的力量，它是推动你向美好生活前进的燃料。

在詹姆·艾伦的文章中，有一段我很喜欢，摘自《命运的主人》：

“所有成功人士都有清晰的理想和目标。他们紧紧把握一个点子，一项工程，或一个计划，绝不让它溜走；珍视它，让它慢慢发芽，呵护它，让它成长；当困难袭来时，他们绝不投降；甚至，追求理想的热情随着遭遇阻碍的强度而愈发增长。”这是值得我们思考的。

32. All You Remember

All you remember about your child being an infant is the incredible① awe you felt about the precious miracle you created. You remember having plenty of time to bestow all your wisdom and knowledge. You thought your child would take all of your advice and make fewer mistakes, and be much smarter than you were. You wished for your child to hurry and grow up.

All you remember about your child being two is never using the restroom alone or getting to watch a movie without talking animals. You recall afternoons talking on the phone while crouching in the bedroom closet, and being convinced your child would be the first Ivy League college student to graduate wearing pullovers at the ceremony②. You remember worrying about the bag of M&M's melting in your pocket and ruining your good dress. You wished for your child to be more independent.

All you remember about your child being five is the first day of school and finally having the house to yourself. You remember joining the PTA and being elected president when you left a meeting to use the restroom. You remember being asked "Is Santa real?" and saying "yes" because he had to be for a little bit longer. You remember shaking the sofa cushions③ for loose change, so the toothfairy could come and take away your child's first lost tooth. You wished for your child to have all permanent④

① incredible[in'kredəbl] *adj.* 难以置信的

② ceremony['seriməni] *n.* 典礼,仪式

③ cushion['kuʃən] *n.* 垫子,软垫

④ permanent['pəːmənənt] *adj.* 永久的,持久的

teeth.

All you remember about your child being seven is the carpool schedule①. You learned to apply makeup in two minutes and brush your teeth in the rearview mirror because the only time you had to yourself was when you were stopped at red lights. You considered painting your car yellow and posting a "taxi" sign on the lawn next to the garage door. You remember people staring at you, the few times you were out of the car, because you kept flexing your foot and making acceleration② noises. You wished for the day your child would learn how to drive.

All you remember about your child being ten is managing the school fund-raisers. You sold wrapping paper for paint, T-shirts for new furniture, and magazines for shade trees in the school playground. You remember storing a hundred cases of candy bars in the garage to sell so the school band could get new uniforms, and how they melted together on an unseasonably warm spring afternoon. You wished your child would grow out of playing an instrument.

All you remember about your child being twelve is sitting in the stands during baseball practice and hoping your child's team would strike out③ fast because you had more important things to do at home. The coach didn't understand how busy you were. You wished the baseball season would be over soon.

All you remember about your child being fourteen is being asked not to stop the car in front of the school in the morning. You had to drive two blocks further and unlock the doors without coming to a complete stop. You remember not getting to kiss your child goodbye or talking to him in front of his friends. You wished your child would be more mature.

All you remember about your child being sixteen is loud music and undecipherable④ lyrics screamed to a rhythmic beat. You wished for your

① schedule[ˈʃedjuːl; ˈskedʒjul] *n.* 时间表,进度表

② acceleration[ækˌseləˈreiʃən] *n.* 加速度

③ strike out *v.* 打,击,冲压成,勾销,产生,做成

④ undecipherable[ˈʌndiˈsaifərəbl] *adj.* 破译不出的,难辨认的

child to grow up and leave home with the stereo.

All you remember about your child being eighteen is the day they were born and having all the time in the world.

And, as you walk through your quiet house, you wonder where they went and you wish your child hadn't grown up so fast.

你所记得的事

当你的孩子是个婴儿时,你所记得的,是你对自己创造出的宝贵奇迹感到不可思议的敬畏。你记得你有大量的时间去传授你所有的智慧和知识。你认为你的孩子将会接受你所有的忠告而少犯错误,将会比孩提时代的你聪明许多。你希望你的孩子快快长大。

孩子两岁时,你所记得的,是孩子从不能独自使用卫生间,从不看一部与动物无关的电影。你记得那些蜷缩在卧室储衣间跟朋友通电话的下午,深信你的孩子将是第一个身着学位服出席毕业典礼的常春藤名牌大学毕业生。你记得你担心那袋 M&M 巧克力糖会在你的衣兜里融化,毁了你体面的衣服。你希望你的孩子更独立些。

孩子 5 岁时,你所记得的,是他上学第一天你终于独自拥有整个房子了。你记得参加家长—教师联系会,在你离开会议室去洗手间时,你当选为会长。你记得孩子问你"圣诞老人是真的吗?"你回答"是的",因为他还需要你的肯定回答,尽管不久他就能自己判断了。你记得在沙发垫子下一通翻腾要找出些零钱,这样牙齿仙女就会来把你孩子掉的第一颗牙带走。你希望孩子的牙都换成了恒牙。

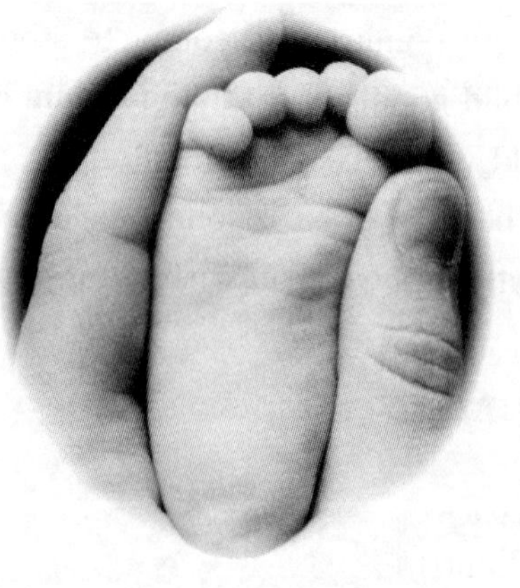

孩子 7 岁时,你所记得的,是合伙用车的时间安排。你学会了在两分钟内化完妆,照着汽车后视镜刷牙,因为你能给你自己找出的时间就只有汽车停在红灯前的那小段。你想过把你的车子漆成黄色,并在车库门旁的草坪上立一个"出租车"的标志牌。你记得有几次你下车后,人们盯着你,因为你不断用脚踩油门加速,制造噪音。你希望孩子有一天能学会开车。

孩子10岁时,你所记得的,是怎么组织学校的募捐者。你们为购置涂料兜售包装纸,为购置新家具兜售T恤衫,为在学校操场上种植遮阳树劝人订阅各种杂志。你记得你在车库里存放了上百盒糖果等待出售,得到钱后学校的乐队就可以购置新制服,可是那些糖果竟在一个暖和得过头的春天的下午全都融化在一起了。你希望孩子长大,不再演奏什么乐器了。

孩子12岁时,你所记得的,是孩子在体育场打棒球练习赛时,你坐在看台上希望你孩子所在的队很快三击不中出局,因为家里还有更重要的事等你去做。教练不明白你为什么那么忙。你希望棒球赛季能尽快结束。

孩子14岁时,你所记得的,是孩子不让你早晨把汽车停在校门口。你不得不开过两个街区,车还没停稳就赶紧打开车门。你记得不再与孩子吻别,或不在他的朋友面前与他谈话。你希望孩子能更成熟些。

孩子16岁时,你所记得的,是吵闹的音乐和以富有节奏的拍子尖声唱出的难以听懂的歌词。你希望孩子快点长大成人,带着音响离开家吧。

孩子18岁时,你所记得的,是他们出生的那一天,拥有世间所有的时光。

当你在静静的房子里走来走去时,你纳闷他们去哪里了——你希望孩子别这么快就长大了。

33. Feed Your Mind

Since the pre-historic times, man has had an urge to satisfy his needs. Be it hunger, shelter or search for a mate, he has always manipulated① the circumstances to the best of his advantages. Probably this might be the reason why we human are the most developed of all living species on the earth, and probably also in the universe. As we climbed the steps of evolution② with giant③ leaps, we somehow left behind common sense and logical thinking—we forgot that we have stopped thinking ahead of times.

If you are hungry, what do you do? Grab a piece of your favorite meal and stay quiet after that? Just like your stomach, even your mind is hungry. But it never lets you know, because you keep it busy thinking about your dream lover, favorite star and many such absurd④ things. So it silently began to heed to your needs and never let itself grow. When mind looses its freedom to grow, creativity gets a full stop. This might be the reason why we all sometimes think "What happens next?", "Why can't I think?", "Why am I always given the difficult problems?" Well this is the aftermath⑤ of our own karma of using our brain for thinking of not-so-worthy things.

Hunger of the mind can be actually satiated⑥ through extensive reading. Now why

① manipulate[mə'nipjuleit] *v.* (熟练地)操作,使用
② evolution[ˌiːvə'luːʃən] *n.* 进展,发展,演变,进化
③ giant['dʒaiənt] *adj.* 庞大的,巨大的
④ absurd[əb'səːd] *adj.* 荒谬的,可笑的
⑤ aftermath['ɑːftəmæθ] *n.* 结果,后果
⑥ satiate['seiʃieit] *v.* 使满足,使饱享

reading and not watching TV? Because reading has been the most educative tool used by us right from the childhood. Just like that to develop other aspects of our life, we have to take help of reading. You have innumerable① number of books in this world which will answer all your "How to?" questions. Once you read a book, you just don't run your eyes through the lines, but even your mind decodes it and explains it to you. The interesting part of the book is stored in your mind as a seed. Now this seed is unknowingly used by you in your future to develop new ideas. The same seed if used many times, can help you link and relate a lot of things, of which you would have never thought of in your wildest dreams! This is nothing but creativity. More the number of books you read, your mind will open up like never before. Also this improves your oratory② skills to a large extent and also makes a significant contribution to your vocabulary. Within no time you start speaking English or any language fluently with your friends or other people and you never seem to run out of the right words at the right time.

Actually, I had a problem in speaking English fluently, but as I read, I could improve significantly. I am still on the path of improvement to quench③ my thirst for satisfaction. So guys do join me and give food for your thoughts by reading, reading and more reading. Now what are you waiting for? Go, grab a book, and let me know!

① innumerable[iˈnjuːmərəbl] *adj.* 无数的,数不清的

② oratory[ˈɔrətəri] *n.* 讲演术

③ quench[kwentʃ] *v.* 结束,熄灭,淬火

充实你的思想

自史前时代起,人类就有了满足自己需求的强烈欲望。无论是饥饿、避难或寻找伴侣,人总是操纵着环境使其达到最利于自己的状态。这或许解答了为什么人类是地球上、甚至是宇宙中最高级的现存物种。然而在进化的阶梯上阔步向前之时,我们却不知何故将一些常识和逻辑思维抛诸脑后了——我们忘记了自己已经停止了超前思维。

如果你饿了,你会怎么做?抓起你最喜爱的美食,吃过之后就静静地待着?而你的大脑像你的胃,也会感到饥饿,但它却从不让你知道,因为你让它一直想着你的梦中情人、你最喜爱的明星和许多诸如此类的荒唐事。因此它只是默默地留意着你的需要,却从不让自己成长。当思维恣意成长时,创造力就戛然而止。这也许就是为什么我们有时会想“下一步该如何”,“为什么我想不到?”,“为什么我总是碰到难题?”的原因吧。这也是我们的大脑总在考虑那些无甚价值的事情产生的后果。

事实上,思维的饥荒可以通过广泛的阅读来满足。为什么是阅读而不是看电视呢?因为自孩提时代起,读书就已经是最具教育性的工具了。正如人生发展的其他方面一样,我们不得不求助于阅读。世界上有无数书籍可以回答你“如何做”的问题。读书时不仅要用眼睛浏览文字,还要用脑去解读、诠释。书中有趣的部分就会像种子一样贮存在你的脑海里。将来你会不自觉地运用这粒种子引发新的想法。多次运用这粒种子将有助于你把许多事情联系起来,即使你做梦都想不到这些!这不是别的,这就是创造力!你读的书越多,你的心智就会前所未有地开阔。而且这还会大幅度地提高你的演讲能力、丰富你的词汇量。你很快就能用流利的英语或别的语言与你的朋友或别人交谈,而且你再也不会在适当的场合缺少适当的词语。

实际上,我的英语还是不够流利,但只要我阅读,我就会取得显著进步。现在我仍在“自我提高”,为头脑“解渴”的长路上跋涉。请加入到我的行列吧!通过阅读、阅读、再阅读来为你的思想“喂食”。你还在等什么?现在就拿起一本书让我瞧瞧!

34. Beauty Life

There were a sensitivity and a beauty to her that have nothing to do with looks. She was one to be listened to, whose words were so easy to take to heart.

It is said that the true nature of being is veiled. The labor of words, the expression of art, the seemingly ceaseless① buzz that is human thought all have in common the need to get at what really is so. The hope to draw close to and possess the truth of being can be a feverish one. In some cases it can even be fatal, if pleasure is one's truth and its attainment② more important than life itself. In other lives, though, the search for what is truthful gives life.

I used to find notes left in the collection basket, beautiful notes about my homilies and about the writer's thoughts on the daily scriptural③ readings. The person who penned the notes would add reflections to my thoughts and would always include some quotes from poets and mystics he or she had read and remembered and loved. The notes fascinated me. Here was someone immersed in④ a search for truth and beauty. Words had been treasured, words that were beautiful. And I felt as if the words somehow delighted in being discovered, for they were obviously very generous to the as yet anonymous⑤ writer of the notes. And now this person was in turn learning the secret of sharing them. Beauty so shines when given away. The only truth that exists is, in that sense, free.

It was a long time before I met the author of the notes.

One Sunday morning, I was told that someone was waiting for me in

① ceaseless[ˈsiːslis] *adj.* 不停的,不断的

② attainment[əˈteinmənt] *n.* 达到

③ scriptural[ˈskriptʃər(ə)l] *adj.* 手稿的,圣经的,依据圣经的

④ immerse[iˈməːs] *v.* 沉浸,使陷入

⑤ anonymous[əˈnɔniməs] *adj.* 匿名的

the office. The young person who answered the rectory door said that it was "the woman who said she left all the notes". When I saw her I was shocked, since I immediately recognized her from church but had no idea that it was she who wrote the notes. She was sitting in a chair in the office with her hands folded in her lap. Her head was bowed and when she raised it to look at me, she could barely smile without pain. Her face was disfigured, and the skin so tight from surgical procedures① that smiling or laughing was very difficult for her. She had suffered terribly from treatment to remove the growths that had so marred her face.

We chatted for a while that Sunday morning and agreed to meet for lunch later that week.

As it turned out we went to lunch several times, and she always wore a hat during the meal. I think that treatments of some sort had caused a lot of her hair to fall out. We shared things about our lives. I told her about my schooling and growing up. She told me that she had worked for years for an insurance company. She never mentioned family, and I did not ask.

We spoke of authors we both had read, and it was easy to tell that books are a great love of hers.

I have thought about her often over the years and how she struggled in a society that places an incredible premium② on looks, class, wealth and all the other fineries of life. She suffered from a disfigurement③ that cannot be made to look attractive. I know that her condition hurt her deeply.

Would her life have been different had she been pretty? Chances are it would have. And yet there were a sensitivity and a beauty to her that had nothing to do with looks. She was one to be listened to, whose words were so easy to take to heart. Her words came from a wounded but loving heart, very much like all hearts, but she had more of a need to be

① procedure[prəˈsiːdʒə] *n.* 程序,手续

② premium[ˈprimjəm] *n.* 额外费用,奖金,奖赏

③ disfigurement[disˈfigəmənt] *n.* 毁容,缺陷,畸形

aware of it, to live with it and learn from it. She possessed a fine-tuned sense of beauty. Her only fear in life was the loss of a friend.

How long does it take most of us to reach that level of human growth, if we ever get there? We get so consumed and diminished, worrying about all the things that need improving, we can easily forget to cherish those things that last. Friendship, so rare and so good, just needs our care—maybe even the simple gesture of writing a little note now and then, or the dropping of some beautiful words in a basket, in the hope that such beauty will be shared and taken to heart.

The truth of her life was a desire to see beyond the surface for a glimpse① of what it is that matters. She found beauty and grace and they befriended her, and showed her what is real.

美丽人生

她有一种与外表无关的灵气和美丽，她的话语很容易征服人心，她正是我们要聆听的声音。

人们说人生的真谛被遮蔽着，词语的费力诠释、艺术的着力表现以及人类那似乎永无休止的纷繁思索都在苦苦追寻人生的真谛。走进和掌握存在真谛的希望可以是十分狂热的。有时候，有些人以自己笃信的真理为志趣，追寻真理甚于保全生命，于是就有舍生取义之举。然而，也有另外的一种人生，他们在追求真谛的过程中获得生命。

我过去常常在教堂的捐款篮里发现小纸条，其中一些文笔优美的纸条是有关我的布道，有些是作者日常读《圣经》的感想。写这些纸条的人不仅对我的一些观点加以反思，同时还会引用一些他或她曾经读过的、令他或她难忘又喜爱的诗人或者神秘主义者的话。我被这些纸条迷住了。我看到了一个执著于追寻真与美的人。其宝贵而又优美的词语让我感到那些字句也乐于让我们发现，它们是那么毫无保留地、慷慨地为这无名氏作者借用，而现在轮到这位无名氏来学习与人分享这些美文的奥秘。分享让美闪耀光辉，在这个意义上说，唯一存在的真理是免费可得的。

过了很久我才见到这些纸条的作者。

① glimpse[glimps] *n.* 一瞥，一看

一个星期天早上，我被告知有人正在办公室等我。帮我应门的年轻人说：“是位女士，说所有的纸条都是她放的。”看见她的时候我大吃一惊，因为我马上就认出她是我的教区信徒，只是我一直不知道那些纸条是她写的。她坐在办公室的一张椅子上，两手相扣在大腿上，低垂着头。在抬头看我的时候，她微笑起来却十分费劲。那是一张破了相的脸，外科手术使她的脸皮绷得紧紧地，笑对她来说也是很困难的。为了去除脸上碍眼的肉瘤，她接受了手术治疗，这令她吃尽了苦头。

那个星期天早上我们聊了一会儿，并决定那周再找个时间一起吃顿午饭。

后来我们不止吃了一顿午饭，而是好几顿。每次一起吃饭的时候她都带着帽子。我想可能是她接受的某种治疗使她掉了不少头发。我们分享了各自生活中的点点滴滴。我跟她讲我读书和成长的故事。她告诉我她在一家保险公司里已经工作多年了。她从来没有提过自己的家庭，我也没有问。

我们还谈到大家都读过的作家的作品，不难发现她非常喜欢看书。

这些年我经常想起她，在这个以外表、地位和财富等虚名浮利挂帅的社会中她是怎样一路挺过来的呢？毁掉的容颜使她怎么也无法变得耀眼迷人。我知道这深深地刺痛着她。

如果她长得漂亮，她的生命轨迹会不会有所不同呢？有可能。不过她有种独特的灵气和美，与外表完全无关。她的话轻而易举地征服了人心，她的话正是我们要聆听的声音。她的隽语出自一颗受过伤却充满爱的心，就像所有人的心一样，只不过她比别人更注重自己心灵的关注，用心去体会生活并从中学习。她拥有一种细腻的美感。她生命里唯一的恐惧就是失去朋友。

我们究竟要花多长时间才能到达如此高度的成熟？能否最终达到还是个未知数呢？我们老觉得身心疲惫，怀才不遇，只顾为眼前的不足忧心忡忡，却忘了珍视一些历史常新的东西。友谊珍贵而美好，只需我们用心呵护，有时候简简单单的表示就已经足够了，比如偶尔写几句话给朋友，或者在篮子里投入一些优美动人的字条，以期大家都能分享，记住美妙的时刻、美妙的感觉。

她生命的真谛就是要透过事物的表面一睹其真正的本质。她发现了美和慈爱，而美和慈爱也待她如友，把生命的真谛呈现给了她。

35. A Promise of Flowers

For my wife and me, money isn't as available① as it used to be. I switched to a more interesting job that paid less. Then baby James came.

You find ways to house and feed yourself for less, but the big ticket stuff is over: vacations in France or Mexico, Friday-night dinners in nifty new restaurants. Even our long holiday weekends are now spent at home.

Through all the downsizing, though, one thing hasn't changed: the flowers. Starburst lilies still crowd one another on the antique blue sideboard. White tulips in a pitcher on the kitchen butcher block, freesia② and daffodils③ on the plank dining-room table, sunflowers on the sill—they're all there. And on Janet's night stand, always a singly pale pink rose rests in a cut-crystal vase. It smells perfect. Over the course of a week, as each new rose opens, a mystery is played out. For three dollars, that mystery is the world's best bargain.

It's my job to buy the flowers. When the sprays begin to droop and scatter petals, I hie to the florist. I ask which flowers will last the longest, wonder which will look best. Sometimes when money is especially tight, the kitchen goes without. Still, whenever Janet's rose begins to brown or petals drop away, a replacement is quickly bought. Every now and then, I keep a running tab④ of the weekly cost: so far, the most it's come to is $17. We can still swing that.

In the beginning, I bought my wife flowers because they surprised her, and she's smile. After the bouquets and roses became more

① available[ə'veiləbl] *adj.* 可用到的,可利用的

② freesia['fri:ʒiə] *n.* [植]小苍兰属植物

③ daffodil['dæfədil] *n.* 水仙花

④ tab[tæb] *n.* 制表,标号

commonplace, she'd still have that brief astonished expression when she unwrapped them—which counts for something. I've seen her step out of hotshot① restaurants with a lesser glow on her face.

Now there are other reasons to buy flowers. Because we've always had them. Because they've become a touchstone against bad things. Because their small, bright presence helps our life smell a lot more like joy than hardship.

Plato believed such small beauties were a privilege of nature. All I know is that by spending a few squeaky② dollars each week to make Janet smile, I smile. Among her flowers, late at night, I sometimes find calm. And in the quiet house—listening to my wife and baby sleep, suspended③ in the still-waiting promise of a future built around a woman and the few things you can love and hold—the flowers still seem beautiful. And, minutes later, more beautiful still.

花的诺言

对于我的妻子和我，钱不像以前一样宽裕了。我换了一个更有趣的工作，但薪水却比以前少了，然后我们的孩子詹姆士就出世了。

在住房和食品上，你想法子节省没有问题，但奢侈点的花销就没有了：不能去法国或墨西哥度假，也不能在星期五的晚上到优雅的新餐馆就餐了，甚至连长周末也是在家里过的。

虽然这些开支都缩减了，但有一件没有改变：那就是买花。绽放的百合仍然一簇簇地摆在蓝色的旧式餐具架上，白色郁金香摆在厨房砧板上的水罐里，小苍兰和水仙花摆在餐厅里的木桌上，向日葵摆在窗台上，它们全在各自的位置上。还有在珍妮特的梳妆台上，总有一支粉色的玫瑰，插在雕花水晶的花瓶里，散发着幽香。每星期都绽放一朵玫

① hotshot[ˈhɔtʃɔt] *n.* 快车，快船，快机

② squeaky[ˈskwiːki] *adj.* 吱吱响的，发轧声的

③ suspended[sʌsˈpendid] *adj.* 暂停的

瑰,这是一个奇迹。对于3元买一个奇迹,绝对是世界上最好的交易。

买花总是我的事,当花枝开始枯萎、花瓣开始散落时,我就赶紧去花店,问哪些花将会持续最长的花期,哪种最漂亮。有时当钱紧的时候,就免去厨房的花,但每当珍妮的玫瑰花变黄或者花瓣开始凋落,我就很快地买一朵替换。我常计算每周买花的开销,到现在为止,最高是每周17美元,这笔钱我们还能花得起。

最初,我给妻子买花,是因为花会使她惊喜,博她一笑。后来花束和玫瑰变得较平常了,但她拆开包装纸的时候,脸上仍会闪过惊喜的表情,这可不平常,通常我们走出豪华餐馆的时候,我也没见她如此兴奋过。

现在买花有了其他的理由。因为我们一直有花,因为花已经成为幸福快乐的标准,因为花朵虽小,却能使人心旷神怡。有了花,生活对于我们来说就是乐趣而不是苦难。

柏拉图认为细微之处的美是一项大自然才能享有的特权。而我知道每周用几美元让珍妮特高兴,我就高兴。深夜里置身于她的花朵中间,我时常会感到安详与宁静。在静静的家中,听着妻子和孩子的酣睡声,等待着那个尚未被实现的承诺,等待着那建筑在一个女人身边,建筑在你能所爱、所拥有的事物周围的未来。花儿看来依然美丽。几分钟后,它们更加美丽。

36. The Young Can't Wait

When you are little, it's not hard to believe you can change the world. I remember my enthusiasm① when, at the age of 12, I addressed the delegates② at the Rio Earth Summit. "I am only a child," I told them. "Yet I know that if all the money spent on war was spent on ending poverty and finding environmental answers, what a wonderful place this would be. In school you teach us not to fight with others, to work things out, to respect others, to clean up ③our mess, not to hurt other creatures, to share, not be greedy. Then why do you go out and do the things you tell us not to do? You grownups say you love us, but I challenge you, please, to make your actions reflect④ your words."

I spoke for six minutes and received a standing ovation. Some of the delegates even cried. I thought that maybe I had reached some of them, that my speech might actually spur⑤ action. Now, a decade from Rio, after I've sat through many more conferences, I'm not sure what has been accomplished. My confidence in people in power and in the power of an individual's voice to reach them has been deeply shaken.

Sure, I've seen some improvements since Rio. In my home city of Vancouver, most people put out their recycling boxes. The organic grocery and cafe on Fourth Avenue is flourishing. Bikes are popular, and

---

① enthusiasm[in'θjuːziæzəm] *n.* 狂热,热心,积极性

② delegate['deligit] *n.* 代表

③ clean up 打扫干净,整理

④ reflect[ri'flekt] *v.* 反射,反映,表现

⑤ spur[spəː] *v.* 刺激

there are a few gas-electric hybrid cars gliding around. But as this new century begins, my twenty something generation is becoming increasingly disconnected from① the natural world. We buy our drinking water in bottles. We ate genetically modified organisms. We drive the biggest cars ever. At the same time, we are a generation aware of the world—of poverty and social imbalance, the loss of biodiversity②, climate change and the consequences of globalization③—but many of us feel we have inherited④ problems too great to do anything about.

When I was little, the world was simple. But as a young adult, I'm learning that as we have to make choices—education, career, lifestyle—life gets more and more complicated. We are beginning to feel pressure to produce and be successful. We are learning a shortsighted way of looking at the future, focusing on four-year government terms and quarterly business reports. We are taught that economic growth is progress, but we aren't taught how to pursue a happy, healthy or sustainable⑤ way of living. And we are learning that what we wanted for our future when we were 12 was idealistic and naive.

Today I'm no longer a child, but I'm worried about what kind of environment my children will grow up in. In Johannesburg the delegates will discuss the adoption and implementation of documents by government. Yes, important stuff. But they did that at Rio. What this meeting must really be about is responsibility—not only government responsibility but personal responsibility. We are not cleaning up our own

① disconnected[ˌdiskəˈnektid] from 与……分开
② biodiversity[ˌbaiədaiˈvəːsiti] *n.* 生物多样性
③ globalization[ˌgləubəlaiˈzeiʃən] *n.* 全球化,全球性
④ inherit[inˈherit] *v.* 继承,遗传而得
⑤ sustainable[səˈsteinəbl] *adj.* 可持续的

mess; we are not facing up to the price of our lifestyles. In Canada we know we are wiping out the salmon① of the West Coast, just as we wiped out cod from the East Coast, but we continue overfishing. We keep driving our SUVs in the city, even though we are starting to feel the effects of climate change—a direct result of burning too much fossil fuel.

Real environmental change depends on us. We can't wait for our leaders. We have to focus on② what our own responsibilities are and how we can make the change happen.

Before graduating from college last spring I worked with the Yale Student Environmental Coalition to draft a pledge for young people to sign. Called the Recognition of Responsibility, the pledge③ is a commitment from our generation to be accountable④ and a challenge to our elders to help us achieve this goal and to lead by example. It includes a list of ways to live more sustainably simple but fundamental⑤ things like reducing household garbage, consuming less, not relying on cars so much, eating locally grown food, carrying a reusable cup and, most important, getting out into nature. Three friends and I will take the Recognition of Responsibility to Johannesburg, where we will meet with South African students and then present the pledge to the World Summit as a demonstration of personal commitment.

But in the 10 years since Rio, I have learned that addressing our leader is not enough. As Gandhi said many years ago, "We must become the change we want to see." I know change is possible, because I am changing, still figuring out what I think, I am still deciding how to live my life. The challenges are great, but if we accept individual responsibility and make sustainable choices, we will rise to the challenges, and we will become part of the positive tide of change.

---

① salmon[ˈsæmən] *n.* 鲑鱼，大麻哈鱼

② focus on 集中

③ pledge[pledʒ] *n.* 保证，誓言

④ accountable[əˈkauntəbl] *adj.* 应负责的，有责任的

⑤ fundamental[ˌfʌndəˈmentl] *adj.* 基础的，基本的

年轻不能等

小时候,不难相信你能改变世界。我记得12岁的那年,在里约地球峰会上,我对代表们说话时的那种热情。我对他们说:“我只是个孩子,但我知道,如果把花在战争上的钱用来消除贫困和解决环境问题,这个地球将会是多么美好的地方。在学校里,你们教我们不要和别人打架,要商量办事,要尊重旁人,要清理干净我们弄脏的地方,不要伤害动物,要分享,不要贪占。那你们为什么去干你们叫我们别干的事?你们成年人说你们爱我们,那我要求你们,请你们做到言行一致。”

我讲了6分钟的话,得到了全体起立热烈鼓掌欢呼。有些代表甚至哭了。那时我想,我可能打动了一些人,我的演说可能真的会激发行动。现在,里约峰会已过去10年,我也耐着性子出席过许多别的会议,但我不敢说有什么成就。对于当权者,对于个人能够说服当权者,我的信心已大为动摇。

的确,自里约峰会以来,我看到了一些改进。在我的家乡温哥华市,多数人家摆出了可供再生利用食品的垃圾箱。第四大街上的食品杂货店和咖啡屋办得红红火火。自行车流行了,街上还有几辆汽电两用车静静驶过。但当新世纪开始时,像我这样20多岁的一代人却越来越和自然界相脱离了。我喝着买来的瓶装水,吃着转基因食品。我们开的车越来越大。同时,我们这一代人意识到全球新问题:贫穷、社会失衡、生物多样性的丧失、气候变化、全球化的恶果,但是我们很多人感到所承袭的问题规模太大,无能为力。

我还小的时候,世界很简单。但进入成年后,我逐渐认识到生活越来越复杂,我们必须在教育、事业和生活方式上做出选择。我们开始感受压力,要生产财富,取得成功。我们所受的教育是对未来的一种短视的看法,视线局限于4年一届的政府任期和季度财经报告。我们受的教育告诉我们:经济增长就是进步,但没人教我们怎样才能有一个快活、健康、可持续的生活方式。我们现在才逐渐知道,我们12岁时所想要的未来是理想主义的和天真的。

今天我不再是孩子了,但我很担心我的孩子们会生长在什么样的环境里。在约翰内斯堡代表们讨论由各国政府通过和履行的一些文件。是的,这很重要。但是他们在里约热内卢也这样做过。这次会议真的要做的是明确责任——不止政府的责任，还有个人的责任。我们没有清理干净我们自己弄脏的地方；我们没有敢于承担我们目前的生活方式所需付出的代价。在加拿大，我们知道我们正在消灭西海岸的鲑鱼，正像我们已经消灭了东海岸的鳕鱼，但我们还在继续过量捕鱼。在城市里我们仍在继续用跑车，虽然我们开始感觉到气候改变的后果——烧太多化石燃料的直接后果。

真正的环境改变有赖于我们自己。我们不能坐着等领导人了。我们必须集中注意我们自己的责任所在，找出改变环境的方法。

去年春天我从大学毕业前，曾和耶鲁学生环境联合会一起起草了一份供年轻人签名的保证书。名叫“承认责任”的这份保证书意在让我们这代人承诺应负起责任，同时向长辈提出挑战，要他们帮助我们实现这个目标并示范领导。保证书上列举了一些更可持续的生活方式——一些简单却又根本的东西，如减少家庭垃圾、减少消费、勿过多依赖轿车、吃本地生长的食物、携带可多次使用的杯子，更重要的是走向大自然。我和3个朋友将把这份“承认责任”保证书带到约翰内斯堡，在那里我们将与南非学生汇合，然后把这份保证书提交给世界峰会，作为个人承诺的一种示范。

但在里约峰会以来的10年中，我懂得了向领导人呼吁是不够的。正像甘地在许多年前所说的：“我们应成为我们想看到的改变的一部分。”我知道改变是可能的，因为我自己正在改变，还正在捉摸新思路。我还正在就如何生活做出决定。我们面对的挑战是巨大的，但如果我们承担个人责任并选择可持续的生活方式，我们就能迎接挑战，成为积极的改变浪潮的一部分。

37. On Meeting the Celebrated

I have always wondered at the passion many people have to meet the celebrated. The prestige① you acquire by being able to tell your friends that you know famous men proves only that you are yourself of small account. The celebrated develop a technique to deal with the persons they come across. They show the world a mask, often an impressive one, but take care to conceal② their real selves. They play the part that is expected from them, and with practice learn to play it very well, but you are stupid if you think that this public performance of theirs corresponds with the man within.

I have been attached, deeply attached, to a few people; but I have been interested in men in general not for their own sakes, but for the sake of my work. I have not, as Kant enjoined, regarded each man as an end in himself, but as material that might be useful to me as a writer. I have been more concerned with the obscure than with the famous. They are more often themselves. They have had no need to create a figure to protect themselves from the world or to impress it. Their idiosyncrasies③ have had more chance to develop in the limited circle of their activity, and since they have never been in the public eye it has never occurred to④ them that they have anything to conceal. They display their oddities because it has never struck them that they are odd. And after all it is with the common run of men that we writers have to deal; kings, dictators,

① prestige[presˈtiːʒ] *n.* 声望,威望,威信
② conceal[kənˈsiːl] *v.* 隐藏,隐蔽,隐瞒
③ idiosyncrasy[ˌidiəˈsiŋkrəsi] *n.* 特质,特性
④ occurred to 想起,想到

commercial magnates① are from our point of view very unsatisfactory. To write about them is a venture that has often tempted writers, but the failure that has attended their efforts shows that such beings are too exceptional to form a proper ground for a work of art. They cannot be made real. The ordinary is the writer's richer field. Its unexpectedness, its singularity②, its infinite variety afford unending material. The great man is too often all of a piece; it is the little man that is a bundle of contradictory elements. He is inexhaustible③. You never come to the end of the surprises he has in store for you. For my part I would much sooner spend a month on a desert island with a veterinary④ surgeon than with a prime minister.

与名人见面

我总想弄明白为什么许多人热衷于见名人。告诉朋友你认识某个名人,由此而来的声望只能证明你自己微不足道。名人个个练就了一套处世高招,无论遇上谁,都能应对自如。他们给世人展现的是一副面具,常常是美好难忘的面具,但他们会小心翼翼地遮盖自己的真相。他们扮演的是大家期待的角色,演得多了,最后都能演得惟妙惟肖。如果你以为他们在公众面前的表演就是他们的真实自我,那你就傻了。

我自己就喜欢一些人,非常喜欢他们。但一般来说,我对人感兴趣不是因为他们自身的缘故,而是出于我工作的需求。正如康德劝告的那样,我从来没有把认识某人作为目的,而是将其当作对一个作家有用的创作素材。比之名流显士,我更加关注无名小卒。

① magnates[ˈmægneits] *n.* 大资本家,巨头,富豪,要人

② singularity[ˌsingjuˈlæriti] *n.* 单一,异常,奇异,奇妙,稀有

③ inexhaustible[ˌinigˈzɔːstəbl] *adj.* 无穷无尽的

④ veterinary[ˈvetərinəri] *n.* 兽医

他们常常显得较为自然真实，他们无需再创造另一个人物形象，用它来保护自己不受世人干扰，或者用它去感动世人。他们的社交圈子有限，自己的种种癖性也就越有可能滋长，因为他们从来没有引起公众的关注，也就从来没有想到过要隐瞒什么。他们会表露他们古怪的一面，因为他们从来就没有觉得有何古怪。总之，作家要写的是普通人。在我们看来，国王、独裁者和商界大亨等都是不符合条件的。去撰写这些人物经常是作家难以抗拒的冒险之举，可为此付出的努力不免以失败告终，这说明这些人物过于特殊，无法成为一件艺术作品的创作根基，作家也不可能把他们写得真真切切。老百姓才是作家的创作沃土，他们或变幻无常，或难觅其二，各式人物应有尽有，这些都给作家提供了无限的创作素材。大人物经常是千人一面，小人物身上才有一组组矛盾元素，是取之不尽的创作源泉，让你惊喜不断。就我而言，如要在孤岛上度过一个月，我宁愿和一名兽医相守，也不愿同一位首相做伴。

38. Mystery of the Bermuda Triangle

Everyone loves a good mystery. They are so popular, in fact, that some people have been known to create their own. Take the strange story of the Bermuda Triangle for example. If you happen to have a map of the world nearby, spread it out on a table in front of you. Find a pen or pencil and a ruler. Good. Now draw a line connecting Bermuda, a group of tiny islands several hundred kilometers off the east coast of the United States, to Puerto Rico, an island on the eastern edge of the Caribbean Sea. Next, draw a line from Puerto Rico to Florida back to Bermuda. If you are following the directions carefully, you have just described on paper what is called the "Bermuda Triangle". This vast portion① of the western Atlantic Ocean was once one of the biggest mysteries of modern times.

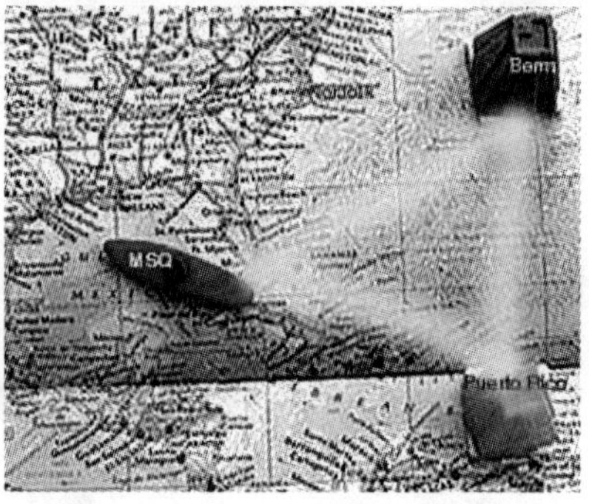

The term "Bermuda Triangle" was the invention of a magazine writer named Vincent Gaddis. Writing in Argosy magazine in 1964, Gaddis talked about the strange disappearance of a large number of ships and planes in this three-sided area of the Atlantic. This one article was enough to get things started. In 1969 a book named *Limbo of the Lost* added more details to the story of this mysterious② part of the ocean. Two years later a feature documentary named *The Devil's Triangle*, dealing with the same subject was released. Ten years after the original magazine article came out the best-selling book *The Bermuda Triangle*, by Charles Berlitz, raised the whole matter up for worldwide attention.

The modern legend of the Bermuda Triangle begins on December 5,

① portion[ˈpɔːʃən] *n.* 部分

② mysterious[misˈtiəriəs] *adj.* 神秘的

1945. On this date five American Navy aircrafts, Flight 19, vanished on a routine training exercise in Florida. Six aircrafts and 27 airmen disappeared without a trace. Articles and books on the disappearance claimed mysterious circumstances. Aircrafts and crewmembers, including one of the rescue aircrafts, had been swallowed up in the dark waters of the Bermuda Triangle. Private investigators and so-called "experts" were soon finding connections to other unexplained ship and aircraft disappearances to this part of the world. Speculation① and guesses became more imaginative as time went on. Some even suggested that the losses were caused by alien life forms living in out space or under the sea in this location.

Others went back in history for more examples of unexplained disappearances and mysterious happenings. Christopher Columbus's journals, some claimed, referred to mysterious lights at sea and unusual compass② readings as they sailed through Bermuda Triangle waters. Another celebrated sea mystery was blamed on the influence of the Bermuda Triangle. In 1892, a ship named Mary Celeste was found floating empty on the ocean. There was no trace of the crew and no clue as to what happened. Finally after all those years an acceptable answer was found. It must have been the Bermuda Triangle.

The Bermuda Triangle, also referred to as the "Devil's Triangle", the "Twilight Zone", and the "Hoodoo Sea", depending on what book or story you were reading, was for a time, the most famous place on earth. Then reality—and groups of real researchers—began to catch up to the claims. The aircraft and men of Flight 19, it turns out, were lost due to a combination of human

① speculation[ˌspekjuˈleiʃən] *n.* 思索

② compass[ˈkʌmpəs] *n.* 罗盘，指南针

errors in navigation① and the failure of electrical systems on the aircraft. The rescue aircraft lost in the search for Flight 19 crashed at takeoff. This fact was simply ignored by creators of the legend. All that was reported about Mary Celeste and the disappearance of her crew was true. What was not mentioned in the Bermuda Triangle stories was that she was found off the coast of Portugal, clearly on the opposite side of the ocean. The strange happenings and sightings on Columbus's ships could have had many explanations. The fact is there were no disappearances or losses in the waters of the Bermuda Triangle.

The measure of a good mystery is whether or not it can stand test of time. Today the Bermuda Triangle mystery has itself all but disappeared. In fact there have been many accidents at sea and in the air in this part of the ocean. It is one of the busiest areas of trade and commerce in the world and many ships and aircrafts pass through the region everyday. It is also an area of active and sometimes dangerous weather systems. Storms and hurricanes② are not uncommon in Bermuda Triangle waters. Accidents happen and sometimes at sea the evidence sinks below the surface without a trace.

【注】

1. Puerto Rico[ˈpwɔːtəuˈriːkəu]:波多黎各,一个位于加勒比海中的美国自治联邦岛,位于希斯巴纽拉岛以东。哥伦布于1493年发现它,16世纪它成为西班牙殖民地,1898年美国—西班牙战争后被割让给美国,1952年宣布为联邦,自60年代起通过各种全民投票保持了其联邦地位,圣胡安是首都和最大城市。

2. Caribbean Sea[kæriˈbi(ː)ən siː]:加勒比海,大西洋西部一海湾,被中南美洲和西印度群岛环绕。自从1914年开通了巴拿马运河,加勒比海便成为重要的航运线之一。该海域的许多岛屿和热带气候使加勒比海成为主要的旅游胜地之一。

① navigation[ˌnæviˈgeiʃən] *n.* 航海,航空,导航

② hurricane[ˈhʌrikən] *n.* 飓风,狂风

百慕大三角的神秘

每个人都喜欢好的神秘故事。实际上,因为它们是那样的受人欢迎,以至于一些人自己制造神秘。拿百慕大三角的奇特故事作个比方吧！如果你碰巧旁边有一张世界地图,请在你面前的桌子上将它摊开,找到一支钢笔或者铅笔和一把尺子。好,现在画一条线,将美国东海岸几百公里处的一群小岛——百慕大,与加勒比海东海角的岛——波多黎各连起来。接着,画一条线,将波多黎各与佛罗里达连起来,再画线回到百慕大。如果你认真地按照这几个方向画,你就在纸上描绘出了被称为“百慕大三角”的地方。这个西大西洋广阔的水域一度是现代最大的神秘之一。

“百慕大三角”这个词是杂志作家文森特·加蒂斯发明的。加蒂斯在1964 年的《大商船》杂志发表的文章中谈到了很多船和飞机在大西洋的三角区域里神秘失踪。这一篇文章就足以挑起整个事件。1969 年,《失踪地带》一书为大西洋这一神秘地区的故事又增加了更多细节。两年后,《魔鬼三角》的纪录片发布着同样的主题。那篇最初的杂志文章发表 10 年后,查尔斯·伯利茨的畅销书《百慕大三角洲》引起了全世界对这件事的广泛关注。

百慕大三角的现代传奇开始于 1945 年 12 月 5 日。这天,5 艘美国海军飞机——飞行 19 号——消失在佛罗里达州的例行训练上。6 艘飞机和 27 名空军消失得无影无踪。文章和书籍声称是神秘失踪。飞机和机组人员——其中包括一艘救援飞机——被百慕大三角的深水吞没了。私人调查者和所谓的“专家”很快联系到了其他轮船和飞机在这里的神秘消失。随着时间的推移,思索和猜测变得越来越富有幻想。一些人甚至说失踪是由于居住在外太空或海洋之下的异类生命形式所引起的。

其他人回顾历史,寻找更多无法解释的失踪和神秘事件。有些声称克里斯多佛·哥伦布的航海日志提到了当他们穿行百慕大三角的水域时,海上有神秘的灯光和指南针的读数非同寻常。另外一件有名的海上神秘事件也归因于百慕大三角的影响。1892 年,一艘名为玛丽·瑟勒斯特的轮船被发现在海洋上空无一人地漂浮着。没有船员的踪迹,也没有关于发生了什么的线索。多年后,一个能够让人接受的答案最后被找到。那一定是百慕大三角。

百慕大三角,也称为"魔鬼三角"、"死亡角"和"魔海",名称取决于你阅读的书籍或者故事,那里一度是地球上最有名的地方。随后,真相——以及一群真正的研究人员——开始跟上传言。实际上,人为的导航失误和飞机上电力系统的失灵共同造成了飞行19号的飞机和机组人员的失踪。寻找飞行19号而失踪的救援飞机在起飞时就坠毁了。这个事实只不过被传奇制造者略去了。所有关于玛丽·瑟勒斯特和她全体船员消失的报道都是真的。在百慕大三角故事里没有提到的是她在葡萄牙海岸上被人发现了,她清晰地出现在海洋的正对面。在哥伦布海船上的奇怪事件和景象可以有很多种解释。事实是在百慕大三角水域里没有失踪或者损失。

验证一个神秘故事的好坏要看它是否能经受时间的考验。今天,百慕大三角的神秘并没有消失。实际上,这片海域上的海上和空中出现过许多意外事故,它是世界上最繁忙的商贸地区之一。每天,许多轮船和飞机通过这一地区。它也是天气系统很活跃、有时又很危险的地区。风暴和飓风在百慕大三角的水域上并不罕见。事故发生后,在海上,证据有时毫无踪迹地沉入海面之下。

39. Monster of Loch Ness

Loch Ness is not one of the most popular places in the world. Hidden away in the Scottish highlands, it is a rugged①, craggy② part of the British Isles with a cool, wet climate that can scare away visitors. In fact Loch Ness might be nothing but unknown to the world were it not for one rather notable attraction. Loch Ness has the distinction of being home to the world's most famous monster.

Loch Ness (Loch is a Scottish word for "lake" or "arm of the sea") is part of what is called the Great Glen, a narrow valley some 96 kilometers long that stretches to the sea from one coast of Scotland to the other. It is one of the three interconnecting lochs in the valley, the other two being Oich and Lochy. Loch Ness is 37 kilometers long, one and half kilometers wide, and 280 meters deep in some places. At its deepest point Loch Ness reaches far below sea level, deeper even than the North Sea.

Despite the reputation of monster as being frightening, dangerous creatures ready to gobble③ up anyone who happens by, the Loch Ness monster seems to have developed a large and popular following in modern times. "Nessie", as the monster is called by her loyal fans, she proved to be neither fearsome nor harmful. In fact Nessie seems to be rather shy and withdrawn, preferring its own company to that of strangers.

Although many sightings of the creature have been recorded, they are no truly reliable images or pictures of her existence. Most accounts of the monster's appearance refer to a very large creature with a long neck and

① rugged[ˈrʌgid] *adj.* 高低不平的，崎岖的，粗糙的

② craggy[ˈkrægi] *adj.* 多峭壁的，崎岖的

③ gobble[ˈgɔbl] *v.* 狼吞虎咽

small head, and flippers, something like those of a whale or fish, for propulsion① through water.

The first encounter② with a monster in Loch Ness was recorded around 1500 years ago. According to the record, an Irish saint, St. Columba, chased away a large and fearful creature that was attacking one of his monks as the monk swam across the loch. The monster, apparently, was frightened off by the shouting of the saint and had no heart to return. There is no record of another sighting until centuries later. In 1871 a Scotsman named Mackenzie described that he saw a strange creature moving slowly across the loch. Others who saw the creature, at the same time, described it as having a large hump on its back that rose out of the water.

Loch Ness monster hunting had become an industry in Scotland in recent times. Modern interest in Nessie began with a sighting that occurred in May of 1933. A local newspaper report of an enormous animal swimming in the loch caused some excitement. London newspaper sent reporters north for stories of a "monster in Loch Ness". A circus owner even offered a £20,000 reward for capturing the monster. (So far the reward has gone unclaimed.)

There has been one famous photograph that claimed to be absolute proof of the Loch Ness monster. This photo, taken in 1934, shows a creature with a long curving neck and small head swimming half submerged③ in the water. The picture was discredited 60 years later, however, when the photographer, in his old age, admitted to faking the photo for a newspaper story. The search for Nessie continues these days with the use of high - tech equipment . In

① propulsion[prəˈpʌlʃən] *n.* 推进,推进力

② encounter[inˈkauntə] *n.* 遭遇,遇见

③ submerge[səbˈməːdʒ] *v.* 浸没,淹没

recent times two deep-sea submersibles①(miniature② submarines③ used for deep water investigations) have been brought in for detailed sonar searches of the Loch. So far, no monster.

With all the time and effort (and all the money) put into the search and no monster to show for it, it is understandable that some people might get a little desperate. In 1975 several creative individuals settled on another approach. Having decided that monster was male, the group designed and built a 94-meter long "Lady Nessie", complete with false eyelashes and makeup, to lure the monster from his hiding place. The lady even gave out a mating call. As you might have guessed, it didn't work. In fact the lady was damaged when they tried to put her into water. And, perhaps regrettably, the shy and mild-mannered monster of Loch Ness never did show up to meet his date.

Of course there has been speculation over the centuries about what the Loch Ness monster really is. Some say the sightings may have been nothing more than seals or large fish in the loch. One theory had it that a creature resembling a species of dinosaur④ could be living somewhere in its depths. Others have suggested that minor volcanic activity at the bottom of the loch could have caused disturbances⑤ in the water that were mistaken for a monster. Guesses range from floating debris to unusual wave pattern on the surface of the water. No explanation accounts for the attraction that has lasted for so long.

Shy, anti-social, or just bored with the foolish games of humans, it doesn't seem to matter. Today Nessie has more websites and more interest on the internet alone, than most rock bands or movie stars will ever have. And a little out-of-the-way corner of Scotland continues to do a thriving business in monster tourism. The legend continues.

① submersible[səbˈməːsəbl] *n.* 潜艇
② miniature[ˈminjətʃə] *adj.* 微型的,缩小的
③ submarine[ˈsʌbməriːn] *n.* 潜水艇,潜艇
④ dinosaur[ˈdainəsɔː] *n.* 恐龙
⑤ disturbance[disˈtəːbəns] *n.* 骚动,动乱

尼斯湖水怪

尼斯湖并不是世界上最有名的地方之一。它远远地藏匿于苏格兰高地，是英伦三岛崎岖不平的地区，气候阴冷潮湿，足以吓走游客。实际上，如果不是因为著名的景点，尼斯湖在世界上则是默默无闻。它享有世界上最有名的水怪在此安家的美誉。

尼斯湖（Loch 在苏格兰语中是“湖”或者“海湾”的意思）是世人称作“大峡谷”的一部分，这个狭窄的峡谷长约 96 公里，从苏格兰的一个海岸延伸到另一个海岸。它是峡谷中三个相连湖泊中的一个，其他两个分别是奥奇和洛奇。尼斯湖长 37 公里，宽 1.5 公里，有些地方深达 280 米。尼斯湖最深的地方远在海平面以下，甚至比北海还深。

尽管水怪的声誉令人害怕，危险的物种随时准备吞掉任何碰巧路过的人，但是，尼斯湖水怪在现代社会似乎成了广为人追寻的对象。她被忠诚的追逐者称作“尼子”，说明了她既不可怕也没有害。其实，尼子似乎很害羞，很孤僻，喜欢独处，不喜欢跟陌生人待在一起。

虽然水怪的可视画面有过记录，但都不是证明她存在的真实可靠的图像或照片。很多关于水怪样子的描述提到她是个脖子长、头小、长着稽状肢的大型物种，稽状肢像鲸或鱼类的翅，在水中推进。

1500 年以前就记录了第一次遭遇尼斯湖水怪的情形。按照这个记录，爱尔兰圣徒哥伦巴赶走了一个大型的、可怕的家伙，当时这个大家伙正在袭击他的一个游过湖面的僧侣。水怪显然被圣人的叫嚷吓坏了，再也不敢回来。一直到几个世纪以后才又有了有人目睹的记载。1871 年，一个名叫马肯兹的苏格兰人描述他看到一个奇怪的生物慢慢地游过湖面。其他同时看过水怪的人描述它的背部有一个能浮出水面的巨大驼峰。

捕猎尼斯湖水怪近年来在苏格兰已经变成了一种产业。现代人对于尼斯湖的兴趣开始于 1933 年 5 月发生的有人目睹的一幕。一份当地报纸报道了一只巨型动物在尼斯湖游泳而引起一些骚动。伦敦的报纸派记者到北方去采写“尼斯湖水怪”的新闻。一位马戏团老板甚至悬赏 20000 英镑来捕获水怪。（迄今为止，这个奖还没有人来领。）

有一张著名的照片声称是关于尼斯湖水怪的绝对证据。拍摄于1934年的这张照片显现出一个脖子又长又弯、头小的生物半淹没在水中。然而，60年后，这张照片被证明是不足为信的，摄影师晚年承认照片是为报纸新闻而伪造的。这些日子来，人们借助高科技设备继续寻找尼子。最近一段时间，两个小型深海潜水艇(用于深水调查的微型潜水艇)已经放进湖中，进行详细的声纳探测。迄今为止，没发现水怪。

大量的时间和精力(还有金钱)投入了搜寻，但水怪并没有出现，难怪有些人会有点绝望。1975年，几个富有创造精神的人达成另一个方法。他们肯定水怪是雄性的，因而设计和建造了一个94米长的“女尼子”，配上假睫毛，加以化妆，去水怪藏身的地方引诱他。这个女水怪甚至还发出了求偶信息。就像你可能猜到的那样，这根本不起作用。事实上，当他们尽力把这个女水怪放入水中时，她就被损坏了。也许遗憾的是，这位害羞和脾气温顺的尼斯湖水怪从来没有现身赴约。

当然，过去的几百年里，人们一直在思索尼斯湖水怪到底是什么。有些人说那些图像只不过是湖里的海豹或大型鱼类。一种理论说某个长得像恐龙的怪物也许生活在湖泊深处的某个地方。其他的人认为湖底小型火山活动引起了在水中的骚动，那可能被误认为水怪。各种各样的猜测包括水面漂浮的残骸和奇特的波纹还在进行。没有任何解释能说清楚人们对水怪的兴趣为何持续了如此之久。

害羞、不合群，或者只是对人类愚蠢的游戏感到厌倦，这些似乎都不重要。今天，尼子比多数摇滚乐队和电影明星都拥有更多的网站，在互联网上激起人们更大的兴趣。苏格兰一个有些偏僻的角落仍然兴旺地做着水怪的旅游生意。传奇还在继续着。

40. My Father Is a Woman

My dad is a woman.

He wasn't always a woman, or else he wouldn't be my dad, but he is one now, and that can make Father's Day difficult. Hallmark simply does not have a department dedicated to transgendered-parent① cards. Most of the Father's Day cards have fishing themes, or refer to other stereotypically manly activities, and say things like "You have a big car, Dad." There's nothing even remotely close to "Dear Dad: You look great in a dress!"

About 20 years ago Dad decided to tell us that what he'd always wanted to be "and deep down inside always had been" was a woman. Like buying a gun, changing one's gender has a waiting period demanded by law, so that when the waiting period is over you can be sure that you really want to do what you were thinking of doing. There are no snap decisions here, which we were grateful ②for, but what Dad decides Dad does, he's very determined that way.

It was a bit confusing for my brother and me, for the obvious reasons, but also for other, less obvious reasons. Twenty-two years ago, Dad seemed like a man's man. He was successful, a vice president of a major company, and like most fathers in the 1960s, not home a lot. He was sort of known for his domineering③, intimidating④ nature, and while Dad didn't like to fish, he did enjoy sailing and skiing; he had a pilot's license, and knew how to build things in that sort of gender-specific male way.

He'd say, "Gee, a fireplace would be nice over there." He'd designed, constructed, and lit it, without any downdraft problems. Dad

① transgendered-parent 变性父母

② grateful['greitful] *adj.* 感激的,感谢的

③ domineering[ˌdɔmi'niəriŋ] *adj.* 极权的,作威作福的

④ intimidating[in'timideitiŋ] *adj.* 胁迫的,令人胆怯的

was a very difficult role model because everything he did was so perfect, almost everything, that is. Coming to think of it, I used to have trouble finding him the right kind of Father's Day card when he was a man too. There was nothing sweet or easy about dear old Dad. In truth, I have always opted for the generic① wish-with-no-frills-attached card that simply said, "Happy Father's Day." Try and find one.

My brother and I have spent hours on the phone trying to figure out what to send Dad for Christmas, his birthday, and, of course, Father's Day. It has gotten better over time, we're older and the shock has worn away, but some years it was just too hard to deal with, especially when we were, essentially, still kids.

The first time when Dad and I talked about the family situation I was 18. He flew me home for the weekend from New York City, where I was studying to become the next Martha Graham. We sat at the picnic table in the backyard while my mother and brother waited inside the house for me. For some reason I felt as if I had been bad and was going to receive a severe talking. The wood from the bench wore into my butt bones as Dad talked about his concerns, the correct terminology "transgender" rather than transsexual.

He seemed very stern as he told me, "I am not like Rocky Horror, or those transvestites② you see in the Greenwich Village Halloween Parade. I am a real woman inside." His real inner name was Ann. I remember looking up at the house and seeing my mother and brother talking in the kitchen. I don't remember much else. I felt alone but did not cry. I flew back to New York City.

Last Christmas we were sitting around the living room, and talking about Dad, which is how we refer to him still. The fire was crackling in the fireplace, Praetorius was playing in the background, and I mentioned how horrible it had been to be flown home for the weekend in order to have my father tell me he was a woman and then to be stuffed back on a

---

① generic[dʒiˈnerik] *adj.* 类的,一般的,普通的

② transvestite[trænsˈvestait] *n.* 异性模仿欲

plane for New York City.

"I think that was the cause of my first nervous breakdown," I told my mother and brother, who have never actually come to terms with the fact that I have had two. Breakdowns and identity crises run in our family. They looked at me as they so often do, wondering if I was joking or seriously disturbed.

"I told you a month before that," my mother informed me. "We were walking down the beach. I was worried about your brother, but I knew you could handle it because you lived in New York City." (My mother thinks that if you live in New York you can handle anything.) "After I told you I asked you for your advice. You were very helpful."

It is extremely disturbing to learn that the way you remember something is not the way it actually happened. It's like an inner earthquake that starts with tremors① and ends with full-scale depression. Something inside of what she had said seemed to fit, though. There were holes around the memory that I had never tried to fill. I knew that dates and weekends did not add up to the events I did remember, but I never tried to reconstruct any of it; it had seemed safer not to. Suddenly those holes weren't empty anymore.

I was 18. I still had crushes on rock'n'roll stars and college seniors. I was barely a woman myself; I was not ready for my father to be one. I have always known that somewhere in the midst of that summer something happened. I lost a part of myself in the Swiss cheese of my mind. And hearing my mother tell me the truth was like flying through the clouds at night and suddenly seeing the lights below, seeing that Earth is much closer than it seemed, and knowing the landing is going to be hard , jarring②, and a

① tremor['tremə] *n.* 震动,颤动

② jarring['dʒɑːriŋ] *adj.* 刺耳的,不和谐的

little disorienting①.

That summer I was studying hard to become a professional dancer and learning that it was not as easy as just making a wish. Mom and I walked along the beach because that is something we always did; we love our mother-daughter walks. She had found out about dad's "problem", as she termed it, when I was 10. I remember that day because it was the first time I ever saw my mother cry, and it frightened me. On the beach, eight years later, I learned why she had been crying. I said something very adult, something like, "It seems like Dad is having an affair with himself." I really helped her, she says.

I still do not recall our conversation. Instead, I am looking through a thin shroud② that covered my consciousness until I was ready to pull it back and look inside. I guess I'm ready now, but lately I've been stumbling into my life, tripping over little things that didn't used to touch me and feeling injured by them. The world has become an awkward place again, and I don't seem to fit inside. I think my father has spent his whole life feeling this way.

Here's what I remember of that summer when I was 18: Trying to choreograph③ a dance and spending hours sitting on the studio floor, not moving a muscle. Looking at the light-bulb hanging from the ceiling in my dorm room and thinking how it looked like solitary confinement④ in a mental institution. Staring out the window all night, unable to sleep and unaware why I could not stop weeping. The stray kitten I'd adopted, watching me from the window, backlit by the moon a calico angel sent to comfort me. Injuring myself. Ignoring newfound friends. Sleeping outside because my dorm room had the residue of lunacy⑤ in it.

I do not remember my mother telling me that my father was

---

① disorient[disˈɔːrient] v. 使失去方向感,使迷惑
② shroud[ʃraud] n. 裹尸布,寿衣,覆盖物
③ choreograph[ˈkɔ(ː)riəgrɑːf] v. 设计舞蹈动作
④ solitary confinement 单独囚禁
⑤ lunacy[ˈljuːnəsi] n. 精神失常,精神病

transgendered, but I know that she did. And when my father finally told me himself, one month later, I was understanding and supportive and normal and went back to New York to my dorm room, my kitten, and the end of memory. This year I went to see my father for the first time since he had the gender reassignment surgery. Even now, as I write this, I can feel the lump in my throat, the tightness in my chest. I know that the stumbling around me comes from this reconciliation①. Some days I feel raw inside, and I still haven't figured it all out in terms of who I am, but the confusion is slowly diminishing. The truth is that I love my father. I am proud of my dad. I feel this all-encompassing empathy② for his pain and discomfort in being a man. I am sorry that he had to go through so many years of pretending to be someone he was not.

Still, I have been furious③ at him for my losses. Maybe I would have been a great choreographer instead of a struggling writer if he had stayed a man. Maybe I would have had a wonderful and magical summer in the city, rather than that nightmare of loneliness. Maybe not. Seeing Dad was the culmination of the earthquake that shook my life 22 years ago. I am still trying to walk in a world where fathers are generally "but not always" men. I am still learning to call Dad "she".

Lately, I have been having dreams where my dad and I are laughing and I feel myself thinking, inside of the dream, "He is really a woman." Dad is happier now. She's retired; she paints all day. She's happier than I have ever seen him, but I realize the real reason is that he is now a she. That's important.

At some point in our lives we want the best for our parents, just as they have wanted the best for us. In truth, I like Dad better as a woman. She's not as threatening, or superior, or domineering. She's an artist with an artist's soul and the most amazing blue eyes, which I never really looked into until now. I have never been a grown-up around my father,

① reconciliation[ˌrekənsiliˈeiʃən] *n.* 和解，调和

② empathy[ˈempəθi] *n.* 移情作用

③ furious[ˈfjuəriəs] *adj.* 狂怒的，狂暴的

but there is still time. There may not be any Father's Day cards for my dad, but there is love of her daughter.

我父亲是个女人

我爸爸是个女人。

他过去并不总是个女人,要不他就不会是我的爸爸,但他现在是,这给父亲节出了个难题。豪玛商店确实没有专门的部门出售献给变性父母的贺卡。多数父亲节贺卡的主题是钓鱼,或是老一套的男人活动,上面说的话都是"爸爸,你有一辆大轿车。"几乎没有一张卡片上隐隐约约提到"爸爸,你穿着裙子真帅!"

大约20年前,爸爸决定告诉我们他"从内心深处一直就是"一位女人,一直想成为一位女人。就像购买枪支一样,改变性别也有法律上要求的等待期,以便等待期过了之后,你才能确信你是否真的要做你想做的事。谢天谢地,这儿没有一时冲动的决定,但是,爸爸决定的事情,他就要做到,他的决心很大。

出于明显或不明显的原因,我和哥哥都感到迷惑不解。22年前,爸爸似乎是男人中的豪杰,事业成功,当上了一家大公司的副总,就像60年代多数父亲那样,他经常不在家。他出了名的天性好管人,办事有魄力。尽管爸爸不喜欢钓鱼,但他确实喜欢航行和滑雪,他有飞行员执照,知道怎样做特别男性化的事情。

只要他说:"嘿,那儿做一个壁炉多好呀。"他就会想方设法去设计,去建造,直到点燃壁炉为止。爸爸是很不简单的那号人,因为他做的一切都是那么完美,我说的几乎所有的东西。现在想一想,当他还是个男人的时候,给他挑选合适的父亲节贺卡我就很犯难。对于亲爱的老爸,没什么有那么甜蜜或轻松。实际上,我总是选择那种祝愿性的而不带花哨的普通卡片,上面只写着"父亲节快乐",试着去找一张吧!

我和哥哥已经打了几个小时的电话了,试图弄清在圣诞节、爸爸的生日,当然还有父亲节,该给爸爸送些什么礼物。随着时间的推移,事情有了好转,我们长得越来越大了,那一惊人的消息已经消失在记忆里了。但是,那些年,尤其是我们还基本

上是个小孩的时候,那件事情太难应付了。

我18岁那年,爸爸第一次跟我谈起家庭状况。他从纽约市——我在那里上学,努力成为第二个舞蹈家玛莎·格拉罕——飞回家度周末,我们坐在后院里的野炊餐桌旁,而妈妈和哥哥在屋里等着我。出于某种原因,我感到好像我做了什么坏事,他们要跟我严肃地谈一谈。当爸爸谈到他的问题——正确的术语该是"变性"而不是"异性转换"——的时候,我感到板凳上的木头扎进了我的股骨里。

跟我谈话时,他显得异常严肃:"我不像罗基·霍偌,或是那些你们在格林尼治村万圣节游行队伍中看到的那些打扮成异性的人。我在内心深处是个真正的女人。"他内心真正的名字叫"安"。我记得我抬头看着房子,看见妈妈和哥哥在厨房里交谈,其他的我记不得了。我感到很孤单,但没有哭出来,第二天就飞回了纽约市。

去年圣诞节,我们围坐在起居室里,谈论着爸爸——我们仍然这样称呼他。壁炉里的火劈劈啪啪地烧着,房间里播放着"蒲拉托里乌斯"音乐,我提到我从纽约大老远地飞回家度周末,就为了听爸爸告诉我他是个女人,然后又将自己塞进飞机里飞回纽约市,这件事情多么可怕呀!

"我想那就是我第一次精神崩溃的原因,"我对妈妈和哥哥说,他们实际上从没有接受我精神崩溃和身份危机二者兼有的事实,此二者正在我家流行。他们就像往常一样看着我,想知道我是在开玩笑还是真的精神错乱。

"我在那之前的一个月就告诉了你,"妈妈对我说,"在我们沿着海滩走着的时候,我就担心你哥哥,但是,我知道你能处理好,因为你住在纽约市。"(妈妈认为如果你住在纽约,你就能处理任何事情。)"我告诉你之后,我问过你的意见,当时你说的话对我很有帮助。"

令人极为烦恼的是,了解到你记忆事情的方式并不是事情真正发生的方式。那就像内心世界里发生的地震,开始是震动,最后是全方位的消沉。虽然妈妈所说的某些话似乎是符合实际情况的。记忆里有我从没有去填满的某些空洞,我知道日期和周末加起来并不等于我所记得的事件,但是我从不特意去重建事实,不那样似乎更好。突然间,那些洞不再是空的。

18岁时,我仍然对摇滚乐歌星和大学高年级学生很着迷。我自己几乎还不是个女人,对爸爸要做女人还没任何准备。我总是记得那个夏日中的某个时候发生了某件事情。在我的脑海里,我已经失去了自己的某个部分。听到妈妈告诉我真相就像夜晚在云端上飞行,突然见到下面的光线,看见地球显得更近,知道着陆会很艰难,刺耳,而且有些迷失方向。

那个夏天,我勤奋学习,想成为一名职业舞蹈家,我发现那不像我许个愿那么容易。我和妈妈沿着海滩走着,因为那是我们经常进行的活动,我们喜欢这种母女一同散步,她已经发现了爸爸的“问题”——我 10 岁的时候,她就这么说的。我清楚地记得那一天,因为那是我第一次看见妈妈痛哭,让我感到很可怕。8 年后,在海滩上,我才知道她为什么哭泣,我说着非常成人化的东西,就像是“爸爸似乎在跟自己发生风流韵事”。妈妈说我真的给了她帮助。

我仍然不记得我们之间的谈话,相反,我尽力看透裹着我意识的一层薄薄的布,直到我准备将它拉回,看看里面是什么样子。我想我现在已经准备好了,但最近,我一直对生活感到困惑,在那些过去与我无关的小事上磕磕绊绊,感到我被它们伤害了。世界又变成了一个令人尴尬的地方,内心里我似乎不适合这个世界,我想爸爸一辈子都有那种感觉。

18 岁的那个夏天,我所记得的就是:我努力地设计一种舞蹈,在舞蹈室的地板上一坐就是几个小时,一动不动的;看着寝室天花板吊着的电灯,想着在精神病院单独监禁会是什么样子;我整晚盯着窗外,不能入睡,不知道我为什么不能停止哭泣;我领养的那只迷路的小猫从窗户那儿看着我,月光映衬着的穿着印花衣裳的天使被派来安慰我。我在伤害自己,不注重新交往的朋友,在户外睡觉,因为我的寝室里遗留着某种精神病。

我不记得妈妈告诉过我爸爸变性了,但我知道她说过。一个月后,当我父亲最后告诉我他的事情,我很理解,也很支持,并很正常地回到纽约市,回到自己的寝室,回到小猫身旁,回到记忆的末端。今年,自从爸爸做了变性外科手术之后,我第一次去看望他。即使到了现在,在我写这篇文章时,我还能感到我喉咙梗塞,胸口沉闷。我知道我自己的困惑就来自这种调和。有些天,我感到内心刺痛,我仍然找不出我是谁的答案。但是,这种迷惑在慢慢消失。事实是我很爱我的爸爸,我为他感到自豪。我感到了他做男人的痛苦和不适。这么多年来他不得不做某个并非是真实的他的人,我为他感到遗憾。

当然,因为我的失落感,我一直对他很愤恨。如果他仍然保持男身,也许我就成了一位伟大的舞蹈指导,而不是辛勤笔耕的作家;也许我在这座城市里度过了一个神奇而又美妙的夏天，而不是孤独的噩梦；也许什么都没有。看望父亲就像是22 年前那场地震的顶点，震撼着我的人生。我仍然走在一个父亲基本上还是男人“但并不总是男人”的世界里；我在努力学会管爸爸叫“她”。

最近，我一直在做梦，梦见父亲和我都在笑，我感到自己在想；在梦里，他是个真正的女人。爸爸现在感到快乐多了，她已经退休了，整天画画。她比以前我见到他的任何时候都快乐，我认识到真正的原因是他现在已经变成了“她”，这很重要。

在我们生活的某一点上，我们都希望我们的父母最好，就像他们希望我们最好一样。实际上，我更喜欢我父亲是个女人，她不是那么威严，不是那么高高在上，不是那么盛气凌人。她是个艺术家，具有艺术家的心灵和最令人着迷的蓝眼睛，直到现在我才看出来。在父亲身旁，我从来就长不大，但我还有时间。可能再也没有为我父亲特制的父亲节贺卡，但是有她女儿对她的爱。

41. My Father's Lessons

My father was one of those old-fashioned country preachers[1] who spouted verses from the pulpit of his little Baptist church and made the listeners tremble in their seats. He could recite whole chapters from John without ever glancing at *The Bible* clutched in his hand.

One afternoon after school, my father and I drove to visit one of the elderly ladies of the congregation[2]. I had just received my new third-grade reader. It was my first real hard cover book and I was very proud of it.

I had already read one story to my father and was starting another one, when I came to a word that I did not know. I held the book up so father could see it and asked him what the word was. He mumbled[3] something about not being able to read and drive at the same time, so very slowly I spelled the word: "a-u-t-u-m-n". My father drove on in silence. Angry, I yelled at him, "Can't you read?"

My father pulled the car over to the side of the road and turned off the ignition[4]. "No, Cathy, I can't read," he whispered softly. "No, I can't read." He reached over and took my new book out of my hand. "I can't read anything in this book." He said with such pain that even I, an eight-year-old child, could feel it.

Very quickly, my father began to talk of his childhood, of the big family that survived by the physical labor of its members. If it was time to harvest the crops, school and books could wait. They had to hoe cotton in

① preacher[ˈpriːtʃə(r)]n. 传教士
② congregation[ˌkɔŋgriˈgeiʃən]n. 集合,集会,[宗]圣会
③ mumbled[ˈmʌmbl]v. 喃喃而语,咕哝
④ ignition[igˈniʃən]n. 点火,点燃

the summer and pick it in the fall. In the winter, they had to slaughter① and preserve animals. There were many mouths to feed, and everyone had to pull his or her load. To make life even more difficult, my father had two brothers who were handicapped, so the others had to double up and do the work they could not. As a result of his excessive② absences from school, my father failed several grades. His motivation to learn evaporated③, and at the age of 16, he dropped out.

I will never forget the sorrow in my father's voice as he told me this story. He seemed so ashamed and saddened to not have been able to help his five children with their lessons in school.

"But Father, how could you read whole chapters of *The Bible* aloud from the pulpit, without ever missing a word?" I asked. He explained that he memorized the passages that my mother read aloud to him over and over. When I heard that, I loved my father more than ever. He was a remarkable man and it was at that moment that I vowed to teach him how to read.

Whatever lessons my teacher gave me at school, I shared with my

father. I taught him the sounds and patterns of languages as I learned them. When I read a story at school, I came home and taught my father to read it. When I struggled with a new concept, he struggled aloud with me, in return he helped me find mnemonic④ devices to memorize items that I needed to pass tests. Soon he learned to write simple stories and poems. Then he was able to write quotations⑤ and jot down notes that he

① slaughter[ˈslɔːtə] *v.* 屠宰,残杀,屠杀
② excessive[ikˈsesiv] *adj.* 过多的,过分的
③ evaporate[iˈvæpəreit] *v.* 蒸发,消失
④ mnemonic[ni(ː)ˈmɔnik] *adj.* 记忆的,记忆术的
⑤ quotation[kwəuˈteiʃən] *n.* 引用语

needed for his sermons①. The proudest moment of my life came when my father read the scripture—really read it for his Sunday sermon.

In 1977 doctors diagnosed my father with terminal② lung cancer, and he died nine months later. During those final months he read *The Bible* from Genesis through Revelation. His proudest moment was when he closed *The Bible*, knowing he could read all that was written inside it.

Before my father died, he thanked me for the gift that I had given him. He didn't realize, however, the gift that he had given me: I knew that just as he was called to be a pastor, I was called to be a reading teacher. Because of my father, I believe that if I can spare one child the heartache and humiliation③ of illiteracy④, my career as a teacher is wholly worthwhile. Thank you, Father!

父亲的课程

我的父亲是位老式的乡村牧师,他能在浸礼会小教堂的讲坛上滔滔不绝地朗诵经文,直到听众坐不住为止。他不看手里攥着的《圣经》也能把《约翰福音》通篇背诵出来。

一天下午我放学后,父亲和我开车去拜访一位同教会的年长女士。我那天刚刚领了三年级的新课本,这可是我第一本硬皮书,我为此非常骄傲。

我给父亲读完了一个故事,就在要开始读第二个故事时,碰到了我不认识的词。我举起书让父亲看,问他是什么意思。他咕哝着说开车时看不清。我便一个字母、一个字母地拼给他听——"a-u-t-u-m-n"。父亲一言不发,只顾开车。我很生气,冲他喊起来:"你难道不识字吗?"

父亲将车停到路边,关掉引擎。"对,凯西,我确实不识字,"他轻声低语地说:"对,我不识字。"他伸手从我手中拿过书。"这本书,我一个字都不认识。"他说话时,表情很痛苦,就连8岁大的我也看得出。

接着,父亲平静地谈起他的童年,他生长在一个大家庭中,家里每个成

① sermon[ˈsəːmən] *n.* 训诫,说教,布道
② terminal[ˈtəːminl] *adj.* 末期的
③ humiliation[hjuːˌmiliˈeiʃən] *n.* 羞辱,蒙耻
④ illiteracy[iˈlitərəsi] *n.* 文盲

员都是做体力活的。每逢秋收,学业就要被耽误。他们必须在夏天播下棉花,在秋天采摘。冬天要宰杀牲畜,并且储藏起来。家里那么多嘴等着吃饭,每个人都负担不轻。更糟糕的是,父亲有两个残疾兄弟,于是其他人便要做双份工来弥补他们做不了的那份。因为缺了很多课,父亲几次留级,于是他读书的信心就化为泡影,在16岁那年退了学。

我永远不会忘记那一刻父亲声音里的悲痛。他显得很惭愧很伤心,因为他不能辅导5个儿女的功课。

“可是爸爸,那您怎么能一字不漏地在讲坛上大声朗诵《圣经》呢?”我问。他解释说是妈妈把文章反复大声念给他听后,他把它们全背了下来。听了这些话后,我比以前更爱我的父亲了。他真的很优秀,从那一刻起,我发誓要教会父亲识字。

老师在学校里教的所有知识,我回家后都和父亲一起分享。我教父亲我所学的发音和句型。在学校读的故事,我回家就教给父亲读。我为了一个新概念绞尽脑汁时,他就和我一块儿大声地讨论。反过来他还帮助我想办法记住考试的内容。很快他学会了写简单的故事和诗歌。然后他能写引语,记下布道时所需的笔记。我人生中最为骄傲的时刻是父亲在星期天布道时念出经文——真正地念出经文。

1977年,医生确诊父亲已是肺癌晚期,9个月后他去世了。在最后的几个月里,他读着《圣经》,从《创世纪》到《启示录》。而他感到最骄傲的时刻是当他合起《圣经》时,他知道自己可以阅读里面所写的内容了。

父亲在去世之前,曾感谢过我为他做的一切。他却没有意识到他赋予我的一切:我知道,正如他成为一位牧师,我也成了一位阅读课教师。因为我父亲,我懂得了只要我能帮助一个孩子摆脱不识字的痛苦和屈辱,我便实现了作为教师的价值。谢谢您,父亲!

42. Can I Buy an Hour of Your Time?

A man came home from work late, tired and irritated, to find his 5-year-old son waiting for him at the door.

"Daddy, may I ask you a question?"

"Yeah sure, what is it?" replied the man.

"Daddy, how much do you make an hour?"

"That's none of your business. Why do you ask such a thing?" the man said angrily.

"I just want to know. Please tell me, how much do you make an hour?" pleaded the little boy.

"If you must know, I make $20 an hour."

"Oh," the little boy replied, with his head down. Looking up, he said, "Daddy, may I please borrow $10?"

The father was furious, "If the only reason you asked that is so you can borrow some money to buy a silly toy or some other nonsense, then you march yourself straight to your room and go to bed. Think about why you are being so selfish. I work hard every day for such childish behavior."

The little boy quietly went to his room and shut the door. The man sat down and started to get even angrier about the little boy's questions. How dare he ask such questions only to get some money? After about an hour or so, the man had calmed down, and started to think: Maybe there was something he really needed to buy with that $10 and he really didn't ask for money very often.

The man went to the door of the little boy's room and opened the door.

"Are you asleep, son?" He asked.

"No daddy, I'm awake," replied the boy.

"I've been thinking, maybe I was too hard on you earlier," said the man. "It's been a long day and I took out my aggravation on you. Here's the $10 you asked for."

The little boy sat straight up, smiling. "Oh, thank you daddy!" He yelled. Then, reaching under his pillow he pulled out some crumpled-up bills. The man, seeing that the boy already had money, started to get angry again. The little boy slowly counted out his money, then looked up at his father.

"Why do you want more money if you already have some?" the father grumbled.

"Because I didn't have enough, but now I do," the little boy replied. "Daddy, I have $20 now. Can I buy an hour of your time? Please come home early tomorrow. I would like to have dinner with you."

我可以买你一小时的时间吗？

一个人工作到很晚,带着疲惫与愤怒回到家里,却发现5岁大的儿子正在门口等他。

"爸爸,我可以问你一个问题吗?"

"当然,什么问题?"这个人回答道。

"爸爸,你一个小时挣多少钱?"

"这不关你的事。怎么问这样一个问题?"父亲生气地说道。

"我只是想知道。请告诉我吧,你一个小时挣多少钱?"小男孩乞求地说。

"真想知道就告诉你吧,我一小时挣20美元。"

"噢,"男孩说着,低下了头。接着,他抬起头来问:"爸爸,我可以借你10美元钱吗?"

父亲生气了:"如果你问这个问题,只是为了借钱买无聊的玩具或其他没用的东西,那就赶紧回你的房间睡觉去。想想你怎么会这么自私。我每天工作这么辛苦,得到的竟是这样幼稚愚蠢的举动。"

小男孩静静地走进自己的房间,关上了门。这个人坐下后,更加为这个男孩的问题生气了。这孩子怎么敢问这样的问题,就为了借些钱吗?大约过了一个小时,他才平静下来,开始想:也许他真的需要这10美元买什么东西呢,他并不是经常要钱花的。

于是这个人走到小男孩的门口,打开了门。

“你睡了吗,儿子?”他问。

“没有,爸爸。我醒着呢,”男孩回答。

“我在想,可能刚才我对你太严厉了,”父亲说:“经过漫长的一天,我把怒气都发到你身上了。这是你要的10美元。”

小男孩坐直了身子,笑了:“噢,谢谢爸爸!”他忍不住呼喊起来。接着,他伸手到枕头底下,拿出一把皱巴巴的钞票。看到男孩已经有钱了,父亲又忍不住要发火。小男孩慢慢地数着钱,然后抬头看着父亲。

“既然你已经有钱了,为什么还要更多的钱?”父亲粗鲁地抱怨说。

“因为我的钱不够,不过现在够了,”小男孩回答,“爸爸,我现在有20美元了。我可以买你一小时的时间吗?请你明天早点下班,我想和你一起吃晚饭。”

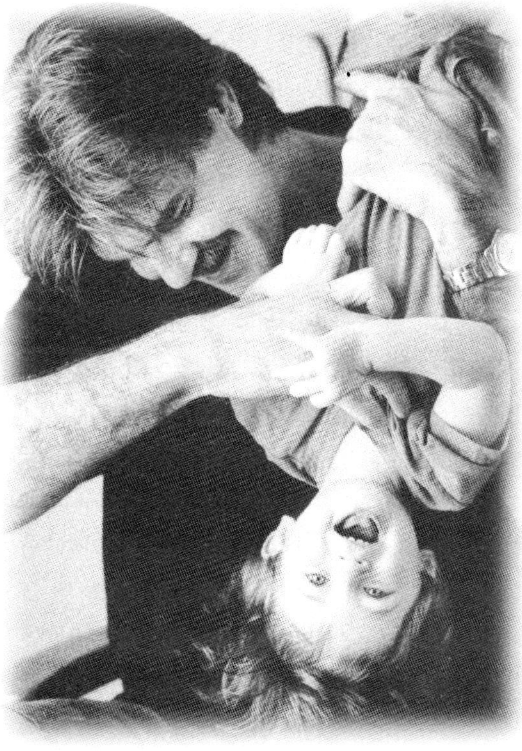

43. Give Us 15 Minutes a Day

Your boss has a bigger vocabulary than you have.

That's one good reason why he's your boss.

This discovery has been made in the word laboratories of the world. Not by theoretical English professors, but by practical, hard-headed scholars who have been searching for the secrets of success.

After a host of experiments and years of testing they have found out:

That if your vocabulary is limited your chances of success are limited.

That one of the easiest and quickest ways to get ahead is by consciously building up your knowledge of words.

That the vocabulary of the average person almost stops growing by the middle twenties.

And that from then on it is necessary to have an intelligent plan if progress is to be made. No haphazard① hit-or-miss methods will do.

It has long since been satisfactorily established that a high executive does not have a large vocabulary merely because of the opportunities of his position. That would be putting the cart before the horse. Quite the reverse is true. His skill in words was a tremendous help in getting him his job.

Dr. Johnson Connor of the Human Engineering Laboratory of Boston and of the Stevens Institute of Technology in Hoboken, New Jersey, gave a vocabulary test to 100 young men who were studying to be industrial executives.

Five years later those who had passed in the upper ten percent all, without exception, had executive positions, while not a single young man

① haphazard[ˈhæpˈhæzəd] *adj.* 没有计划的,任意的

of the lower twenty-five per cent had become an executive.

You see, there are certain factors in success that can be measured as scientifically as the contents of a test-tube, and it has been discovered that the most common characteristic of outstanding success is "an extensive knowledge of the exact meaning of English words".

The extent of your vocabulary indicates the degree of your intelligence. Your brain power will increase as you learn to know more words. Here's the proof.

Two classes in a high school were selected for an experiment. Their ages and their environment were the same. Each class represented an identical cross-section of the community. One, the control class, took the normal courses. The other class was given special vocabulary training. At the end of the period the marks of the latter class surpassed those of the control group, not only in English, but in every subject, including mathematics and the sciences.

Similarly it has been found by Professor Lewis M. Terman, of Stanford University, that a vocabulary test is as accurate a measure of intelligence as any three units of the standard and accepted Stanford-Binet I. Q. tests.

The study of words is not merely something that has to do with literature. Words are your tools of thought. You can't even think at all without them. Try it. If you are planning to go down town this afternoon you will find that you are saying to yourself: "I think I will go down town this afternoon." You can't make such a simple decision as this without using words.

Without words you could make no decisions and from no judgments whatsoever. A pianist may have the most beautiful tunes in his head, but if he had only five keys on his piano he would never get more than a fraction of these tunes out.

Your words are your keys for your thoughts. And the more words you have at your command the deeper, clearer and more accurate will be your thinking.

A command of English will not only improve the processes of your mind. It will give you assurance; build your self-confidence; lend color to your personality; increase your popularity. Your words are your personality. Your vocabulary is you.

Your words are all that we, your friends, have to know and judge you by. You have no other medium for telling us your thoughts—for convincing us, persuading us, giving us orders.

Words are explosive①. Phrases are packed with TNT. A simple word can destroy a friendship, land a large order. The proper phrases in the mouths of clerks have quadrupled② the sales of a department store. The wrong words used by a campaign orator have lost an election. For instance, on one occasion the four unfortunate words, "Rum, Romanism and a Rebellion" used in a Republican campaign speech threw the Catholic vote and the presidential victory to Grover Cleveland. Wars are won by words. Soldiers fight for a phrase. "Make the world safe for Democracy." "All out for England." "V for Victory." The "Remember the Maine" of Spanish war days has now been changed to "Remember Pearl Harbor".

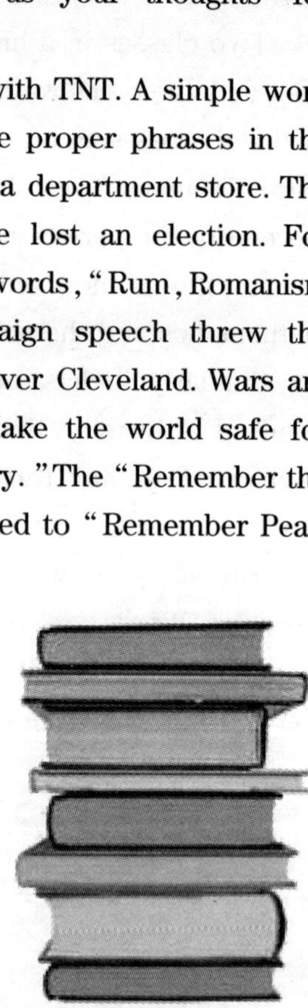

Words have changed the direction of history. Words can also change the direction of your life. They have often raised a man from mediocrity③ to success.

If you consciously increase your vocabulary you will unconsciously raise yourself to a more important station in life, and the new and higher position you have won will, in turn, give you a better opportunity for

① explosive[iks'pləusiv]*adj.* 爆炸性的

② quadruple['kwɔdrupl]*v.* 使成四倍;以四乘

③ mediocrity[ˌmiːdi'ɔkriti]*n.* 平庸;平凡;平庸的人

further enriching your vocabulary. It is a beautiful and successful cycle.

Come to read a book every day. Put a book by your bedside, if you like. A short time spent on these pages before you turn the lights out each night is better than an irregular hour now and then. If you can find the time to learn only two or three words a day—we will still promise you that at the end of thirty days you will have found a new interest. Give us fifteen minutes a day, and we will guarantee, at the end of a month, when you have turned over the last page of the book, that your words and your reading and your conversation and your life will all have a new and deeper meaning for you.

For words can make you great!

每天只需15分钟

你老板的词汇量比你的词汇量大。

这是他为什么会成为你老板的一个重要原因。

这一发现是在世界各地的语言实验室里得来的。它不是那些持有理论的英语教授信口胡诌的,而是那些一直以来就在探讨着成功的秘诀、精明而又讲求实际的学者们发现的。

在经历了大量的试验和多年的验证之后,他们发现:

如果你的词汇量不大,你成功的机会也就不多。

最简洁而又最迅速的改进方法之一就是有意识地扩大你的词汇知识。

普通人的词汇量到了二十五六岁左右就几乎停止增长了。

从那以后要想继续扩大词汇量就必须有一个精心设计的计划。随意安排的、漫无目的的方法是不起作用的。

长期以来人们就有个想当然的看法:高级行政管理人员不会有很大的词汇量,因为在那个位置上,他有的是机会。这未免有点本末倒置了。实际情况恰恰相反。他的言语技巧对他获得那个职位有着巨大的帮助。

约翰逊·康纳博士为波士顿的人才管理实验室和新泽西州霍博肯市的史蒂文斯理工学院工作,他曾对100名学工业行政管理的年轻人做过一次词汇测试。

五年以后那些在考试中名列前十位的人全部地、无一例外地跨上了管理岗位,而考试中位列后25名的人中没有一个能当上管理人员。

你瞧,有一些成功的因素是要以像试管里的物质那样被精确测量的,而人们发现,获得杰出成就的一个最普遍的要素就是"大量而准确地掌握英语词汇"。

你对词汇的把握程度反映了你的智力水平,当你通过学习掌握了更多的词汇的时候,你大脑的思维能力也会增强。以下事例就可以证明这一点。

一所高中的两个班被挑选来做了一个试验。年龄相仿,所处的环境相同。每个班都代表着整个社会的一个完全相当的横截面。其中一个班被作为参照班,只上普通班应上的课程。另一个班则附加特别的词汇训练。到试验期结束的时候,后一个班的成绩,不论是英语成绩,还是每一科的成绩,包括数学和自然学科成绩全都超过了参照班的成绩。

无独有偶,斯坦福大学的路易斯·M.特曼教授也发现,词汇测试与三套普遍被人接受的斯坦福·宾尼特标准智商测试题中的任何一套一样,可以准确地测定智力。

词汇学习并非只是某种与文学有关的事情。词汇是思维的工具。没有了词汇你甚至根本无法思维。你可以试一试。如果你打算今天下午进城,你会发现你在对自己说:"我想今天下午我要进趟城。"不借助词的话,你就连这样一个简单的决定也做不了。

没有了词汇你什么决定也做不了,什么判断也做不成。一位钢琴家的脑袋中可能想到了一首美妙的曲子,但是如果他的钢琴上只有五个音键的话,他永远也只能演奏出这首曲子的一些破碎的片段。

你的词汇是你思维的关键。你所掌握的词汇越多,你的思想就越深邃、越清晰、越准确。

掌握英语不仅可以改进你的思维方式,它还给你信心,令你自信,带给你鲜明的个性,使你更受欢迎。你的用词反映了你的个性。所谓词如其人。

作为你的朋友,我们大家都是从你的言辞中来了解你和评价你的。除此以外,你无法用别的什么交际手段来告诉我们你的想法——无法使我们信服,无法劝服我们,无法给我们下命令。

单词是具有破坏性的。词组中则充斥着火药。一个简简单单的词可以摧垮一份友谊,可以使一大批订货泡汤。售货员言辞得体的话可以使商场的销售额翻两番。况选演说者用词失当则会使他竞选失利。例如,在一次共和党的竞选学说中,因演讲者不慎将"离奇古怪、罗马天主教教义和叛乱"等词连在了一起,结果罗马天主教徒都投了格洛弗·克利夫兰的票,让他赢得了总统竞选的胜利。战争也要靠言语来获胜。战士们往往为一句口号而战。"为保卫世界民主而战。""一切为了英格兰。""必胜。"西班牙内战时代的口号是"牢记缅因河",如今已换成"牢记珍珠港"了。

词汇曾改变过历史的方向。词汇也能改变你生活的方向。它们常常使一个平凡之辈迈向成功。

如果你在有意识地增加着你的词汇量,你将在不知不觉中爬到一个更显要的位置上,得到这个新的、更高的位置以后,反过来,你又会有更好的机会进一步丰富你的词汇量。这是一个诱人的、带给人成功的循环过程。

每天都读一会儿书吧。如果你喜欢的话,就在枕边放一本书。每天晚上关灯之前花一点时间读上几页书要比时不时不定期地花上个把小时来读要好。即使你每天只腾得出时间学两到三个单词——我们仍可向你保证,30 天以后你将会得到新的兴趣。如果你每天花上 15 分钟的话,我们就可以保证,一个月之后,当你翻过了这本书的最后一页时,你的词汇,你的阅读能力,你的谈话技巧,乃至你的生活都将会达到一个更新和更高的程度。

因为词将使你卓越不凡!

44. Loving with an Open Hand

The other day as I talked with a friend I recalled a story that I heard this summer. "A compassionate① person, seeing a butterfly struggling to free itself from its cocoon, and wanting to help, very gently loosened the filaments② to form an opening. The butterfly was freed, emerged from the cocoon, and fluttered about but could not fly. What the compassionate person did not know was that only through the birth struggle can the wings grow strong enough for flight. Its shortened life was spent on the ground; it never knew freedom, never really lived."

I call it learning to love with an open hand. It is a learning which has come slowly to me and has been wrought③ in the fires of pain and in the waters of patience. I am learning that I must free the one I love, for if I clutch④ or cling⑤, try to control, I lose what I try to hold.

If I try to change someone I love because I feel I know how that person should be, I rob him or her of a precious right, the right to take responsibility for one's own life and choices and way of being. Whenever I impose my wish or want or try to exert⑥ power over another, I rob him or her of the full realization of growth and maturation. I limit and prevent by my act of possession, no matter how kind my intention.

I can limit and injure by the kindest

---

① compassionate[kəmˈpæʃənit] *adj.* 有同情心的

② filament[ˈfiləmənt] *n.* 细丝,丝状体

③ wrought[rɔːt] *v.* (work 的过去式和过去分词)铸造,锤炼

④ clutch[klʌtʃ] *v.* 抓住

⑤ cling[kliŋ] *v.* 黏着,紧紧握住

⑥ exert[igˈzəːt] *v.* 施加(压力);行使(职权)

acts of protection or concern. Over extended it can say to the other person more eloquently① than words, "You are unable to care for yourself; I must take care of you because you are mine. I am responsible for you."

As I learn and practice more and more, I can say to the one I love: "I love you, I value you, I respect you and I trust that you have the strength to become all that it is possible for you to become—if I don't get in your way. I love you so much that I can set you free to walk beside me in joy and in sadness. I will share your tears but I will not ask you not to cry. I will respond to your needs. I will care and comfort you, but I will not hold you up when you can walk alone. I will stand ready to be with you in your grief and loneliness but I will not take it away from you. I will strive to listen to your meaning as well as your word, but I shall not always agree. Sometimes I will be angry and when I am, I will try to tell you openly so that I need not hate our differences or feel estranged②. I can not always be with you or hear what you say for there are times when I must listen to myself and care for myself, and when that happens I will be as honest with you as I can be."

I am learning to say this, whether it be in words or in my way of being with others and myself, to those I love and for whom I care. And this I call loving with an open hand.

I cannot always keep my hands off the cocoon, but I am getting better at it!

放爱一条生路

前几天和一位朋友闲聊时,我想起今年夏天听到的一个故事:"有个人很富有同情心,看到一只蝴蝶拼命挣扎想冲破茧的束缚,就帮了个忙,轻轻地解开茧丝使其露出一个缺口。蝴蝶得到解放,从茧中出来振翅欲飞,然而却飞不起来。这位富有同情心的人所不知道的是,只有经过挣扎破茧而出,

① eloquently[ˈeləkwəntli] *adv.* 雄辩地,有说服力地

② estrange[isˈtreindʒ] *v.* 使疏远,使隔离

翅膀才能变得强壮,可以飞翔。这只蝴蝶短暂的生命只能在地上度过了,它从未尝过自由的滋味,没有真正享受过生活。”

我把它叫做学会放爱一条生路。这个教训经历了痛苦的锻造和耐心的洗礼,我才逐渐认识到。我学会了必须给所爱的人自由,如果我抓得太紧、紧握不放、设法控制,结果可能会失去我所想抓住的。

如果我试图改变所爱的人,仅仅因为我觉得他/她应该这样,就等于是掠夺了他/她的一项珍贵的权利,即他/她对自己生命的责任权和生活方式的选择权。无论何时我把自己的意志和权力强加给别人,都会导致他/她无法完全成长和成熟。无论我的意图多么善良,我的控制行为还是限制和阻碍了他们。

即使保护或关心这种最善意的行为也会限制和伤害别人。“你无法照顾自己,我必须照顾你,因为你是我的,我要对你负责。”对别人说这么动人的语言远远超越了你的权力。

随着我学习和锻炼的增多,现在我会这样告诉我爱的人:“我爱你,珍惜你,尊重你,我相信你有足够的实力发展成为你想要成为的人——如果我不阻碍你的话。我是那么爱你,所以我给你自由,和我共享欢乐与悲伤。我会和你一起流泪,但我不会要求你停止哭泣。我会满足你的需要,关心你,安慰你,但在你能够独立行走时我不会阻挡你。我会时刻准备好,在你悲伤和孤独时站到你身边,但我不会把你的悲伤和孤独带走。我会尽力理解你的话语及其中含义,但不会总是赞同。有时我会生气,当我生气时,我会尽量坦率地告诉你,这样我就不会对我们之间的分歧怀恨于心,产生疏远的感觉。我无法时刻与你在一起,或者听你诉说,因为有时我需要倾听自己,关心自己,当这些发生时,我会尽量如实告诉你。”

对于那些我所爱和所关心的人,我正在学习这样表达,无论是用语言,还是用我对待他人及自己的方式,我把这种方式叫做放爱一条生路。

我不会总把双手从茧的身旁移开,但我正在逐渐进步!

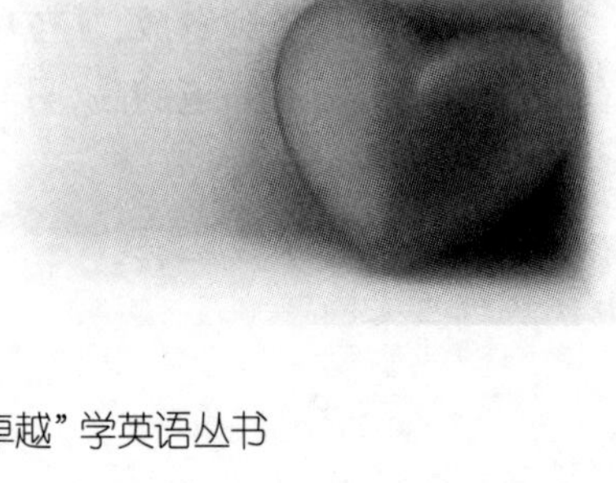

45. Advice to Young People

On Achieving Success

We cannot travel every path. Success must be won along one line. We must make our business the one life purpose to which every other must be subordinate.

I hate a thing done by halves. If it be right, do it boldly. If it be wrong, leave it undone.

The men of history were not perpetually① looking into the mirror to make sure of their own size. Absorbed in their work they did it. They did it so well that the wondering world saw them be great, and labeled them accordingly.

To live with a high ideal is a successful life. It is not what one does, but what one tries to do, that makes a man strong.

"Eternal vigilance②," it has been said, "is the price of liberty." With equal truth it may be said, "Unceasing effort is the price of success." If we do not work with our might, others will; and they will outstrip③ us in the race, and pluck the price from our grasp.

Success grows less and less dependent on luck and chance.

Self-distrust is the cause of most of our failures.

The great and indispensable④ help to success is character. Character is a crystallized⑤ habit, the result of training and conviction⑥. Every character is influenced

① perpetually[pə'petjuəli] *adv.* 永恒地,终身地
② vigilance['vidʒiləns] *n.* 警戒,警惕
③ outstrip[aut'strip] *v.* 超过
④ indispensable[ˌindis'pensəbl] *adj.* 不可缺少的,绝对必要的
⑤ crystallized['kristəlaizd] *adj.* 明确的
⑥ conviction[kən'vikʃən] *n.* 深信,确信

by heredity①, environment and education. But these apart, if every man were not to be a great extent the architect of his own character, he would be a fatalist, and irresponsible creature of circumstances.

Instead of saying that man is a creature of circumstance, it would be nearer the mark to say that man is the architect of circumstance. From the same materials one man builds palaces, another hovels. Bricks and mortar are mortar and bricks, until the architect can make them something else.

The true way to gain much is never to desire to gain too much.

Wise men don't care for what they can't have.

On Happiness

I have never been basically pessimistic②, although I have appeared so to some readers.

I have taken life so seriously as to be disposed to optimism.

Pessimism is a waste of force—the penalty③ of one who doesn't know how to live.

Happiness is in action, and every power is intended for action.

I have always found that it's more painful to do nothing than something.

Of all the virtues, cheerfulness and enthusiasm are the most profitable.

Enthusiasm flourishes more often in adversity④ than it does in prosperity⑤.

Contentment⑥ grows out of an inward

---

① heredity[hi'rediti] n. 遗传

② pessimistic[ˌpesi'mistik] adj. 悲观的，厌世的

③ penalty['penlti] n. 惩罚，刑罚

④ adversity[əd'vəːsiti] n. 不幸，灾祸，逆境

⑤ prosperity[prɔs'periti] n. 繁荣

⑥ contentment[kən'tentmənt] n. 满意，知己

superiority① to our surroundings.

We fall into the mistake of supposing that to look forward must mean to look anxiously forward. It is just as easy to look forward with hope as with sadness.

The source of nearly all the evil and unhappiness of this world is selfishness. We know it; but we still keep on being selfish.

Fame without happiness is but a sorry at best.

给年轻人的忠告

关于取得成功

我们不可能每条路上都走一段，若想成功就必须执著于一条路，我们必须有个毕生的追求，其他皆从属于此。

我痛恨做事半途而废。只要是对的，就要大胆地去做；如果是错的，就不要去做。

名垂青史的人并不是靠终日凝视镜子来衡量自己的形象。他们的形象来自对事业的不懈努力与追求。他们表现出众，于是世界看他们觉得伟大，并就此命名他们为伟人。

成功的人生要具有崇高的理想。一个人是否强大，不在于他做了什么，而在于他努力想做什么。

有人说，"恒久的警惕是自由的代价。"那我们也可以说，"不懈的努力是成功的代价。"如果我们不全力工作，别人就会这样，于是他们将超越我们，抢先摘取胜利的果实。

仅靠运气和机遇，成功会越走越远。

不自信往往导致失败。

成功不可缺少的辅助因素是性格。性格是一种固定的习惯，是不断培养并坚信于此的结果。性格要受到遗传、环境和教育的影响。但除此之外，如果人不能在一定程度上构筑自己的性格，就会成为宿命论者，由此成为环境的失败造物。

① superiority[sju(ː)piəri'ɔriti] *n.* 优越，高傲

与其说人是环境的造物,还不如说人是环境的建筑师。相同的材料,有些人拿来建造宫殿,有些人却只能盖小屋。砖瓦只是砖瓦,建筑师可以把它们变成其他东西。

要想得到更多的办法是永远不要奢望太多。

聪明人不会为他们不能拥有的东西而烦恼。

关于幸福

我基本上从不悲观,尽管有时在一些读者的眼里如此。

我对待生命严肃认真,所以倾向乐观。

悲观纯粹是浪费精力——是对不知道怎样生活的人的惩罚。

快乐在于行动,每一份力量都意在行动。

我总是发现无所事事比工作更痛苦。

所有美德中,愉悦和热情最宝贵。

热情通常滋生于逆境,而非顺境。

满足源自对周围环境的内在优越感。

我们错误地认为,向前看就意味着焦虑地观望,其实向前看能看到忧伤,同时也能看到希望。

自私几乎是世界上所有罪恶与不幸的源头。我们深知这点,却仍继续自私下去。

光有虚名而没幸福,至多也能算作一种遗憾。

46. Trust

Last night I was driving from Harrisburg to Lewisburg, Pa., a distance of about eighty miles. It was late. I was late and if anyone asked me how fast I was driving, I'd have to plead the Fifth Amendment to avoid self-incrimination①. Several times I got stuck behind a slow-moving truck on a narrow road with a solid white line on my left, and I was clinching my fists with impatience.

At one point along an open highway, I came to a crossroad with a traffic light. I was alone on the road by now, but as I approached the light, it turned red and I braked to a halt. I looked left, right and behind me. Nothing. Not a car, no suggestion of headlights, but there I sat, waiting for the light to change, the only human being for at least a mile in any direction.

I started wondering why I refused to run the light. I was not afraid of being arrested, because there was obviously no cop around, and there certainly would have been no danger in going through it.

Much later that night, after I'd met with a group in Lewisburg and had climbed into bed near midnight, the question of why I'd stopped for that light came back to me. I think I stopped because it's part of a contract we all have with each other. It's not only the law, but it's an arrangement we have, and we trust each other to honor it: we don't go through red lights. Like most of us, I'm more apt to be restrained from doing something bad by the social convention that disapproves of② it than by any law against it.

It's amazing that we ever trust each

① self-incrimination[ˈselfˌinkrimiˈneiʃən] *n.* 自证其罪

② disapprove of 不同意

other to do the right thing, isn't it? And we do, too. Trust is our first inclination①. We have to make a deliberate decision to mistrust someone or to be suspicious or skeptical. Those attitudes don't come naturally to us.

It's a damn good thing too, because the whole structure of our society depends on mutual② trust, not distrust. This whole thing we have going for us would fall apart if we didn't trust each other most of the time. We do what we say we'll do; we show up when we say we'll show up; we deliver when we say we'll deliver; and we pay when we say we'll pay. We trust each other in these matters, and when we don't do what we've promised, it's a deviation③ from the normal. It happens often that we don't act in good faith and in a trustworthy manner, but we still consider it unusual, and we're angry or disappointed with the person or organization that violates the trust we have in them.

I was so proud of myself for stopping for the red light that night.

信　任

昨天晚上，我驾车从哈里斯堡驶往宾夕法尼亚州的刘易斯堡，其间距离约80英里。天色已晚。我迟到了，如果有人问我行驶速度有多快，我得求助于美国宪法的第五条修正案，不要自证有罪。我好几次被堵在一辆开得缓慢的卡车后面，路面很窄，而且我左边是不可超越的白线，于是我按捺不住地捏紧双拳。

在公路的某一处，我行驶到了有交通灯的一个十字路口。这时路上只剩下我一个了，但当我快到路口时，交通灯变成了红灯，于是我刹了车。我向左、向右、向后看了看，毫无动静。没有车子，也没有车灯的影儿，但我就那么坐在那儿，等着红灯变绿，方圆一英里内就我一个人。

我开始想，为什么我不闯红灯呢？我不怕被抓着，因为很明显周围并没有警察，闯红灯肯定也不会有任何危险。

① inclination[ˌinkliˈneiʃən] *n.* 倾向，爱好

② mutual[ˈmjuːtjuəl] *adj.* 相互的，共有的

③ deviation[ˌdiːviˈeiʃən] *n.* 背离，偏离

那天夜里,我在刘易斯堡会见了一些朋友,接近午夜时上床后,我又回想起了我为什么要停下来而不闯过去呢。我想,我停了下来,是因为它是我们相互间的一种公约。它不仅是法律,也是我们的一种安排,我们相互信赖,并尊重这一规则:我们不闯红灯。像大多数人一样,我善于克制自己,不做社会行为准则不许做的坏事,而不仅是因为有法律禁止它。

我们从来都是彼此信任会做正确的事,这难道不令人惊奇吗?我们也的确是这样的。信任是我们的第一本能。要让我们不信任某人,猜疑,不相信,那是非常不容易的,因为这种态度对我们很不自然。

这也是一件很好的事情,因为我们整个社会结构是靠互相信任而不是猜疑来维系的。如果我们大部分时间互不信任,那么整个社会秩序将崩溃。我们说到做到;我们说什么时候到场,就什么时候到场;我们说什么时候交货,就什么时候交货;我们说什么时候付款,就什么时候付款。在这些问题上,我们互相信任,要是我们违约的话,那是不正常的。虽然我们常发生不守信用的事,但我们仍认为这是不正常的;对有负我们对其信任的个人或组织,我们感到生气或失望。

我为那天晚上没有闯红灯而感到骄傲。

47. Whatever Love Means—Diana

Although neither of them remembered the occasion①, Diana first met her future husband when she was just a baby. It happened during the winter of 1961, when twelve-year-old Charles, Prince of Wales, was visiting his mother's Sandringham retreat②.

At the time, young Prince Charles barely③ glanced at the tiny baby sleeping in her cot. After all, how could a twelve-year-old boy be interested in babies?

But the Prince would eventually④ take a very keen interest in this particular baby—it would just take some time.

In fact, it would be sixteen years before Prince Charles and Lady Diana Spencer took place in the middle of a farmer's field during a shooting party in November 1977.

It was a cold, rainy, bleak afternoon when sixteen-year-old Diana, dressed in a borrowed parka⑤ that was too large for her, boots, and blue jeans, crossed the field to meet the heir to the British throne.

It was almost twilight when the two came face to face near Nobottle Woods.

"What a sad man," Diana thought when she first saw him. The future Princess was intrigued to finally meet the most eligible⑥ bachelor⑦ in England, though she was not impressed with his

① occasion[ə'keiʒən] *n.* 场合,时机,机会
② retreat[ri'triːt] *n.* 静居处
③ barely['bεəli] *adv.* 仅仅,刚刚,几乎不能
④ eventually[i'ventjuəli] *adv.* 最后,终于
⑤ parka['pɑːkə] *n.* 皮制大衣
⑥ eligible['elidʒəbl] *adj.* 符合条件的,合格的
⑦ bachelor['bætʃələ] *n.* 单身汉

five-foot-ten-inch height, thinking to herself that she would tower over him in high heels. But Diana would later say that she admired his beautiful blue eyes.

The Prince later remarked that he thought Diana was "a very jolly and attractive" girl, "full of fun", though Diana herself believed that "he barely noticed me at all".

Diana, it was discovered later, first came to the attention of the royal family when she acted as a bridesmaid for her sister Jane's wedding that April. It was the first major social occasion that Diana attended as a young woman. And many of the royals were surprised at how beautiful and mature the once-gawky① girl had become.

Even the Queen Mother, Prince Charles's grandmother, noticed Diana's beauty, grace, and charm. She complimented② the Earl on the fine job he had done in bringing Diana up.

A short time later, Prince Charles sent his valet③ to hand-deliver a formal invitation for Diana to accompany him that very evening to the opera and a late night dinner at the palace.

Though she was fluster④, and the invitation came at such short notice, Diana accepted. She and her roommate, Carolyn Bartholomew, hurried to dress and prepare Diana for her big date. The evening was a success, and an invitation to party on the royal yacht⑤ came soon after...

① gawky[ˈɡɔːki] *adj.* 迟钝的,笨拙的
② compliment[ˈkɔmplimənt] *v.* 称赞,褒扬
③ valet[ˈvælit] *n.* (男人的)贴身男仆
④ fluster[ˈflʌstə] *v.* 使慌张,使激动
⑤ yacht[jɔt] *n.* 游艇

Although she was intimidated① by the crowd at Balmoral, Diana was wise enough not to stay in the castle itself. She asked for, and was granted, an invitation to stay with her sister Jane and her young husband at their cottage on the Balmoral estate.

The Prince visited Diana there every day, offering to escort② her to a barbecue③, or extending an invitation for a long walk in the woods.

When Charles went to Switzerland for a ski vacation, Diana missed him terribly. He called her after a day or two, and told Diana he had something important to ask her.

He arrived home on February, 3, 1981. Three days later, he arranged to see Diana at Windsor Castle. Later that evening, while Prince Charles was showing Diana the nursery, he asked her to marry him.

To his surprise, Diana treated his proposal④ as a joke. She actually giggled. But soon she could see that Prince Charles was serious. Despite an insistent⑤ voice inside her head that told her she would never be Queen, she accepted his proposal.

Diana told Prince Charles over and over that she loved him.

"Whatever love means." Was his reply.

爱就是一切——黛安娜

尽管两人都记不得那段往事，可当黛安娜初次与她未来的丈夫邂逅时，她还只是个孩子。那是在1961年的冬天，当时12岁的威尔士王储查尔斯正在夏丁汉他母亲的休养所游玩。

那时，年轻的查尔斯王子对那个睡在童床里的小不点儿瞟都没有瞟一眼。毕竟，12岁的孩子怎么会对婴儿感兴趣呢？

然而，这位王子最终对这个特别的婴儿产生了浓厚的兴趣——只不过

① intimidate[inˈtimideit] *v.* 胁迫

② escort[isˈkɔːt] *v.* 护送

③ barbecue[ˈbɑːbikjuː] *n.* 吃烤烧肉的野餐

④ proposal[prəˈpəuzəl] *n.* 求婚

⑤ insistent[inˈsistənt] *adj.* 坚持不懈的

那是后来的事了。

实际上,查尔斯王子与黛安娜·斯宾塞女士再次邂逅已是16年后的事情了。那次邂逅是在1977年11月的一次乡村狩猎会途中。

那是一个阴雨绵绵、寒风刺骨的下午,16岁的黛安娜,身穿借来的一件过大的毛皮风雪大衣,足蹬长靴,下身是一件蓝色牛仔裤。她正经过这片狩猎场时邂逅了这位英国王位继承人。

接近黄昏时分,二人迎面邂逅在诺布托树林附近。

当黛安娜第一眼看到王子时,心里想:"多么忧郁的一个人。"尽管黛安娜对于他五英尺十英寸的身高并不在意,觉得要是她穿着高跟鞋肯定会高过他,但这位未来的王妃还是期盼与英国最令人中意的单身汉见面。可是黛安娜后来说她很仰慕王子那双迷人的蓝眼睛。

虽然黛安娜自己认为"他根本没注意到我",但王子后来说他觉得黛安娜是个"快乐而迷人的"姑娘,"很有趣"。

人们后来发现,黛安娜第一次引起皇室的注意就是在那年4月她姐姐简的婚礼上,当时她是伴娘。这是她成年后参加的第一个大型社交活动,在许多皇室成员眼里她曾经还是个粗俗难看的丫头,而今却出落成一位如此成熟美丽的女人,他们颇感惊讶。

就连查尔斯王子的祖母王后陛下都注意到了黛安娜的美丽、端庄和迷人。她对伯爵对黛安娜的精心培养倍加称赞。

不久之后,查尔斯王子派随从送给她一张正式的邀请函,邀请黛安娜当晚陪伴他去看歌剧然后出席宫廷晚宴。

尽管黛安娜感到局促不安,并且邀请函来得如此匆忙,可她还是接受了。她与她的室友卡洛琳·巴赛洛缪匆匆忙忙地为自己梳洗打扮准备去赴

这个重大约会。当晚他们玩得非常尽兴,邀请她参加皇家游艇聚会的邀请函不久又接踵而至……

虽然黛安娜对于拜尔马洛的众王族感到有些害怕,可她十分明智没有前往城堡。她提出请求,并得到批准,邀请她住在姐姐简和简的年轻丈夫在拜尔马洛的别墅中。

王子每天都去那里拜访她,要么提出陪她参加户外烤肉宴,要么邀请她去

小树林中散步。

查尔斯去瑞士做滑雪旅行时,黛安娜对他朝思暮想。查尔斯到那里一两天后就打电话给她,告诉黛安娜他回英格兰后,要问她一些重要的事情。

1981年2月3日他回来了。3天后,他安排在温莎堡见黛安娜。那天晚上晚些时候,当查尔斯王子陪黛安娜参观育婴室的时候,他向她求婚。

令王子惊讶的是,黛安娜把他的求婚当作了一个玩笑。她咯咯地笑起来。但后来她看得出查尔斯王子是认真的。尽管她的脑海中一直有个声音告诫她不要想着去当王妃,可她还是接受了王子的请求。

一遍又一遍地,黛安娜诉说着对王子的爱。

"爱就是一切。"王子回答。

48. Detour to Romance

Located in the checkroom[1] in Union Station as I am, I see everybody that comes up the stairs.

Harry came in a little over three years ago and waited at the head of the stairs for the passengers from the 9:05 train.

I remember seeing Harry that first evening. He wasn't much more than a thin, anxious kid then. He was all dressed up and I knew he was meeting his girl and that they would be married twenty minutes after she arrived.

Well, the passengers came up and I had to get busy. I didn't look toward the stairs again until nearly time for the 9:18 and I was very surprised to see that the young fellow was still there.

She didn't come on the 9:18 either, nor on the 9:40, and when the passengers from the 10:02 had all arrived and left, Harry was looking pretty desperate[2]. Pretty soon he came close to my window so I called out and asked him what she looked like.

"She's small and dark," he said, "and nineteen years old and very neat in the way she walks. She has a face," he said, thinking a minute, "that has lots of spirit[3]. I mean she can get mad but she never stays mad for long, and her eyebrows come to a little point in the middle. She's got a brown fur, but maybe she isn't wearing it."

I couldn't remember seeing anybody like that.

He showed me the telegram he'd received: ARRIVE THURSDAY. MEET ME STATION. LOVE LOVE LOVE LOVE. MAY. It was from Omaha, Nebraska.

"Well," I finally said, "why don't you phone to your home? She's probably called there if she got in ahead of you."

① checkroom[ˈtʃekruːm] *n.* 衣帽寄放处

② desperate[ˈdespərit] *adj.* 令人绝望的

③ spirit[ˈspirit] *n.* 个性

He gave me a sick look. "I've only been in town two days. We were going to meet and then drive down South where I've got a job. She hasn't any address for me. "He touched the telegram.

When I came on duty the next day he was still there and came over as soon as he saw me.

"Did she work anywhere?"I asked.

He nodded. "She was a typist. I telegraphed her former boss. All they know is that she left her job to get married."

Harry met every train for the next three or four days. Of course, the railroad lines made a routine① checkup and the police looked into the case. But nobody was any real help. I could see that they all figured that May had simply played a trick on him. But I never believed that, somehow.

One day, after about two weeks, Harry and I were talking and I told him about my theory. "If you'll just wait long enough," I said, "you'll see her coming up those stairs some day. "He turned and looked at the stairs as though he had never seen them before.

The next day when I came to work Harry was behind the counter of Tony's magazine stand. He looked at me rather sheepishly② and said, "Well, I had to get a job somewhere, didn't I?"

So he began to work as a clerk for Tony. We never spoke of May anymore and neither of us ever mentioned③ my theory. But I noticed that Harry always saw every person who came up the stairs.

Toward the end of the year Tony was killed in some argument over gambling, and Tony's widow left Harry in complete charge of the magazine stand. And when she got married again some time later, Harry bought the stand from her. He borrowed money and installed④ a soda

① routine[ruːˈtiːn]*n.* 例行公事,常规,

② sheepishly[ˈʃiːpiʃli]*adv.* 忸怩地,局促不安地

③ mention[ˈmenʃən]*v.* 提及,说起

④ install[inˈstɔːl]*v.* 安装,安置

fountain and pretty soon he had a very nice little business.

Then came yesterday. I heard a cry and a lot of things falling. The cry was from Harry and the things falling were a lot of dolls and other things which he had upset while he was jumping over the counter. He ran across and grabbed a girl not ten feet from my window. She was small and dark and her eyebrows came to a little point in the middle.

For a while they just hung there to each other laughing and crying and saying things without meaning. She'd say a few words like, "It was the bus station I meant" and he'd kiss her speechless and tell her the many things he had done to find her. What apparently① had happened three years before was that May had come by bus, not by train, and in her telegram she meant "bus station", not "railroad station". She had waited at the bus station for days and had spent all her money trying to find Harry. Finally she got a job typing.

"What?" said Harry. "Have you been working in town? All the time?"

She nodded.

"Well, Heavens. Didn't you ever come down here to the station?" He pointed across to his magazine stand. "I've been there all the time. I own it. I've watched everybody that came up the stairs."

She began to look a little pale. Pretty soon she looked over at the stairs and said in a weak voice, "I never came up the stairs before. You see, I went out of town yesterday on a short business trip. Oh, Harry!" Then she threw her arms around his neck and really began to cry.

After a minute she backed away and pointed very stiffly② toward the north end of the station. "Harry, for three years, for three solid years, I've been right over there working right in this very station, typing, in the office of the stationmaster."

① apparently[əˈpærəntli] *adv.* 显然地
② stiffly[ˈstifli] *adv.* 顽固地

浪漫曲折路

我工作的地方就在联合车站的行李寄存处，每一个上楼的人都让我尽收眼底。

大约三年前，哈里来到这里，站在楼梯口等待 9 点 05 分到达的火车上的旅客。

我还记得那是第一次见到哈里时的情景。那时的他，瘦弱不堪，神情焦虑，简直就像个孩子。他穿戴整齐，我知道他是在等女朋友，而且在她到达 20 分钟之后他们就要步入婚姻的殿堂。

旅客们过来了，我得忙碌起来。等到 9 点 18 分的时候我才再往楼梯方向看去，我吃惊地发现那个年轻人还在那里。

她没乘 9 点 18 分的那趟车来，9 点 40 分的车上也没她。等 10 点 02 分那趟车的旅客全都到达并离开后，哈里显得很绝望。不久后他走近我的窗口，我就给他打招呼，问她长得什么模样。

“她身材矮小，皮肤黝黑，”他说，“19 岁，走路的样子很利落。她的脸，”他想了一会儿，说，“很有个性。我的意思是说她会生气，但从不会生气太久。她的眉心处有一个小点儿。她有一件褐色毛皮大衣，不过可能没穿着。”

我想不起来看见过有谁长得像那样。

他给我看他收到的电报：星期四到。车站接我。爱爱爱爱。——梅。电报寄自内布拉斯加州的奥马哈市。

“呃，”我最后说，“你干吗不往家里打个电话？如果她比你先到达这里，她可能已给你家打过电话。”

他懊恼地看了我一眼。“我到城里才两天。我们打算见面之后开车去南方，我在那儿找到了一份工作。她也没给我任何地址。”他摸了摸电报。

第二天我去值班时他还在那儿。一看见我，他就走了过来。

“她在哪儿工作过吗？”我问。

他点了点头。“她本来是个打字员。我给她以前的老板拍了电报。他们只知道她辞了职，结婚去了。”

在后来的三四天里哈里接了每趟车。当然,铁路方面作了例行检查,警察也参与了这件事。但是实际上谁也没帮上忙。我看得出来,他们都推测梅只不过是跟他开了个玩笑,但不知怎么我却根本不这么认为。

有一天,大约是过了两周之后,我和哈里聊天时对他谈了我的想法。“假如你等的时间够长的话,”我说,“总有一天,你会看见她走上楼梯的。”他转过身看着楼梯,仿佛过去从来没见过似的。

第二天我去上班时,哈里已经站在托尼杂志摊的柜台后面了。他不大好意思地看着我说,“呃,我总得在哪儿找个工作,是不是?”

于是,他开始给托尼卖杂志。我们再也不谈梅,谁也不提我的看法。但是我注意到哈里总要关注着每个上楼的人。

到年底时,托尼由于赌博发生争执而被别人杀害了。托尼的妻子将杂志摊完全交给了哈里打理。过了一段时间,她再婚,哈里就从她那儿把杂志摊买了过来。他借了钱,装了个冷饮柜,不久小生意就红火起来了。

后来到了昨天,我听见了一声叫喊,还听见好多东西掉到地上。是哈里在叫喊。掉在地上的是一大堆玩具和其他的东西,都是他跳过柜台时弄翻的。他从这些东西上面跑过去抓住了一个女孩,她就在离我窗户不到10英尺的地方。她个子小小的,黑黑的,眉心处有一个小点。

好一会儿的时间他们就那么待着,相对着笑呀,哭呀,讲些没什么意义的话。她好像说“我指的是汽车站——”而他则把她吻得说不出话来,告诉她自己为找她所做的许多事情。显然,3年前梅是乘汽车而不是火车来的。她电报里指的是“汽车站”而不是“火车站”。她在汽车站等了好几天,为找哈里花掉了所有的钱。最后,她找了一份打字的工作。

“什么?”哈里说,“你在城里工作?一直都在?”

她点了点头。

“哎呀,天哪——你就从来没有来过这个车站?”他把手指向杂志摊。“我一直就在那儿。那个摊儿是我的。我一直关注每个上楼的人。”

她的脸色开始变得有些苍白。过了一会儿,她向楼梯看去,声音微弱地说:“我过去一直没上这个楼梯。你看,我昨天出城是去办点公事——噢,哈里!”然后,她伸手搂住他的脖子,真的哭了起来。

过了一会儿,她往后一站,用手直指车站的最北头。“哈里,3年来,整整3年,我就在那儿——就在这个车站工作,在站长办公室里,打字。”

49. Youth

Youth is not a time of life; it is a state of mind; it is not a matter of rosy cheeks, red lips and supple[1] knees; it is a matter of the will, a quality of the imagination, a vigor of the emotions[2]; it is the freshness of the deep springs of life.

Youth means a tempera[3]—mental predominance[4] of courage over timidity[5], of the appetite for adventure over the love of ease. This often exists in a man of 60 more than a boy of 20. Nobody grows old merely by a number of years. We grow old by deserting our ideals.

Years may wrinkle the skin, but to give up enthusiasm[6] wrinkles the soul. Worry, fear, self-distrust bows the heart and turns the spring back to dust.

Whether 60 or 16, there is in every human being's heart the lure of wonder, the unfailing childlike appetite of what's next and the joy of the game of living. In the center of your heart and my heart there is a wireless station: so long as it receives messages of beauty, hope, cheer, courage and power from men and from the Infinite, so long are you young.

When the aerials[7] are down, and your spirit is covered with snows of cynicism[8]

---

① supple['sʌpl] *adj.* 柔软的
② emotion[i'məuʃən] *n.* 情感,感情
③ tempera['tempərə] *n.* 蛋彩画(用蛋清代油调和的鸡蛋水胶养料画法)
④ predominance[pri'dɔminəns] *n.* 优势
⑤ timidity[ti'miditi] *n.* 胆怯
⑥ enthusiasm[in'θjuːziæzəm] *n.* 狂热,热心,积极性
⑦ aerial['εəriəl] *n.* 天线
⑧ cynicism['sinisizəm] *n.* 犬儒主义,玩世不恭

and the ice of pessimism, then you are grown old, even at 20, but as long as your aerials are up, to catch waves of optimism, there is hope you may die young at 80.

青　春

青春不是似水年华,而是一种心态;青春不是桃面、朱唇、柔膝,而是深沉的意志,丰富的想象力,炽热的情感;青春是生命中充满活力的暗涌。

青春气贯长虹,勇敢超越怯弱,进取压倒苟安。这种气魄,常见于二十几岁的青年,六旬老人则更多见。年岁有加,并非老去,理想放弃,方至暮年。

岁月的风霜吹皱了肌肤;抛却热情定会颓废灵魂。烦忧,惊恐,丧失自信,定会使心灵扭曲,使斗志化为尘土。

无论年届花甲的老人,抑或二八芳龄的少年,心中皆向往生命的欢乐,奇迹的诱惑,他们孩童般天真久盛不衰。人人心中皆有一无线电台,只要你从天上人间接收美好、希望、欢乐、勇气和力量的信号,你就会青春永驻,风华正茂。

一旦天线下降,你的精神便被世俗的不恭冰封、自暴自弃油然而生,即使你年方二十,也已渐渐老去;然而只要你将天线直起,捕捉乐观的电波,即使你在八十高龄告别尘寰,希望犹存。

50. Challenges to Love and Marriage

*Of all the misconceptions about love, the most powerful and pervasive*① *is the belief that falling in love is love or at least one of the manifestations*② *of love.*

—M. SCOTT PECK

People who are married or in committed relationships are healthier, wealthier, and happier. So why do more than 60 percent of marriages end in divorce? Why has the national divorce rate climbed more than 200 percent in the last thirty years? And why are fewer people getting married today than ever before?

The answers to these questions are plentiful, but the main reason is simple. It's easy to "fall" in love, but very few people know how to stay in love. Even though staying in love is our "smartest" choice all the way around! Recent studies on marriage prove it's one of the major ingredients in life-long success for men and women. "It lengthens life, substantially③ boosts④ physical and emotional health, and raises income over that of single or divorced people or those who live together," reported an article in the *New York Times*. Marriage has also been found to boost happiness, reduce the degree of depression, and provide protection from sexually transmitted⑤ diseases.

So let's wake up, make up, and turn this trend around! One of the most startling⑥ pieces of evidence that shows

① pervasive[pəːˈveisiv] *adj.* 普遍深入的
② manifestation[ˌmænifesˈteiʃən] *n.* 显示，表现
③ substantially[səbˈstænʃ(ə)li] *adv.* 充分地
④ boost[buːst] *v.* 推进
⑤ transmit[trænzˈmit] *v.* 遗传，传播
⑥ startling[ˈstɑːtliŋ] *adj.* 令人吃惊的

people are not in touch with what's really going on in their partnerships is the fact that the majority of people who file for divorce say they didn't think there was a relationship-threatening problem just six months prior to breaking up. Another shocker is that most couples wait six years or more to seek professional help when their relationship is in danger. By the time they do wake up and smell the coffee, it's often too late.

Truly there is no reason to resign yourself to a bad relationship whether you're dating or married. Rather than changing partners and ending up this same predicament① again, you can learn to have a fabulous relationship with the partner you already have! I strongly encourage you to make the relationship you have work, because there is a higher rate of divorce and adultery② in second marriages.

Getting rid of your partner does not get rid of the problem, because half of the "problem" is yours. You can walk out on your marriage, but you can't run away from yourself, no matter how hard you try! Rather than blaming each other, couples can learn how to work as a team and coach each other through the troubled times and power struggles. To do this, you must create a "safe" relationship so you can express your needs and fears and effectively resolve③ anger and conflict. More relationships break up because people don't know how to validate④ each other (that frustration escalates⑤ to become anger) than for any other reason. This is truly a shame, because the skills for "fighting fair" are very easy to master with just a little practice and patience⑥.

One of the biggest causes of unresolved anger between people is a

① predicament[pri'dikəmənt] n. 困境
② adultery[ə'dʌltəri] n. 通奸,通奸行为
③ resolve[ri'zɔlv] v. 解决
④ validate['vælideit] v. [律]使有效,使生效,确认,证实
⑤ escalate['eskəleit] v. 逐步升高
⑥ patience['peiʃəns] n. 耐性,忍耐

lack of understanding. Men and women have different strengths and weaknesses, different ways of expressing ourselves, and different "childhood wounds" that we're trying to heal. While it may seem like we're from different planets we are actually very much alike when it comes to our need and desire for love and intimacy①. We only behave differently in our quests for② closeness. Stop doing what you think is "fair" or "right" and start doing what works! It's not about "working harder" it's about "working smarter".

爱情和婚姻的挑战

"在所有有关爱的误解中,影响最大、最深入人心的想法就是爱上某人的'爱'才称之为真正的爱,抑或至少是爱的一种表现。"

——斯科特·派科博士

既然结了婚或者是确定恋爱关系的人更健康,更富有,更幸福,那么,为什么60%的婚姻以破裂而告终?为什么离婚率较之过去的30年会以两倍的速度急剧上升?为什么较之过去越来越少的人步入婚姻的殿堂?

这些问题的答案颇多,而最主要的原因很简单。太容易陷入爱恋,却鲜有人知道如何让爱保鲜,即使"保鲜"也是我们一直以来最好的选择。有关婚姻的最近一项研究表明:婚姻是使男人和女人长久成功的主要原因。《纽约时报》上的一篇文章写到:"婚姻延年益寿,最主要的是加速身体和精神的健康,较之单身和离婚的人,那些一起生活的人的收入要高得多。"据发现,婚姻还可以加速幸福,减少忧郁的程度,并为性传播疾病提供了保护。

因而,让我们清醒清醒,彼此包容,逆转这一潮流吧!事实上,大多数申请离婚的人声称他们在关系破裂之前的6个月里并不存在威胁婚姻关系的问题,这一让夫妻双方对彼此关系

① intimacy[ˈintiməsi] *n.* 亲密
② quest for 追求,探索

感到莫名其妙的证据的确令人吃惊。更令人震惊的是,许多夫妻在他们的关系陷入危机的五六年之后才会寻求专业帮助。他们真正意识到这种危机的时候,已经太迟。

当然,你没有理由将自己束缚在糟糕的关系之中无论你正在约会还是已婚。与其换一位伴侣抑或再次结束这种进退维谷的困境,还不如学会和你原来的伴侣如何和谐相处。我强烈建议你们维持好现有的关系,因为第二次婚姻的离婚率和犯通奸行为的机会更高。

摆脱你的伴侣并不能真正解决存在的问题,因为“问题”的一半归咎于你。你可以走出婚姻,但是你无法逃避自己,无论你做出怎样的努力!与其相互抱怨,夫妻双方不如学会步调协调,相互学习度过生活的种种难关。为了做到这一点,你们应该创造“安全的”婚姻关系,这样你就可以表达你的需要和恐惧,有效地解决愤怒和冲突。许多婚姻关系的破裂无非就是因为夫妻双方不晓得如何验证彼此(沮丧往往升级为愤怒),而非其他原因。这真的很令人感到羞耻,因为“为公平而战”的技巧,仅仅需要一点点实践和耐心就能轻而易举地掌握。

两人之间难以解决的愤怒的最主要的原因之一就是彼此缺乏理解。男人和女人都有不同的强弱点,不同的表达自己的方式,以及我们一直努力治愈的不同的“孩童时期的创伤”。当我们需要并渴求爱情和亲密时,尽管我们看起来来自不同的星球,但实际上我们十分相似。只是因为我们在寻求亲密的关系时表现不同而已。不要再去想萦绕心头的所谓的“公平”和“正义”了,开始做些改善彼此关系的事情吧!并非让你“干得更努力”而是“干得更灵活”。